Hastings Rashdall

Doctrine and Development

University Sermons

Hastings Rashdall

Doctrine and Development
University Sermons

ISBN/EAN: 9783744746632

Printed in Europe, USA, Canada, Australia, Japan

Cover: Foto ©Lupo / pixelio.de

More available books at **www.hansebooks.com**

DOCTRINE AND DEVELOPMENT

UNIVERSITY SERMONS

BY

HASTINGS RASHDALL, D.C.L., M.A.
FELLOW AND TUTOR OF NEW COLLEGE, OXFORD
AUTHOR OF "THE UNIVERSITIES OF EUROPE IN THE MIDDLE AGES"

METHUEN & CO.
36 ESSEX STREET, W.C.
LONDON
1898

TO

MY EARLIEST THEOLOGICAL TEACHER

THE VERY REV.

HENRY MONTAGU BUTLER, D.D.,

MASTER OF TRINITY COLLEGE, CAMBRIDGE

THIS VOLUME IS DEDICATED

IN AFFECTIONATE

GRATITUDE

PREFACE

THIS volume is intended as a modest attempt to translate into the language of modern thought some of the leading doctrines or ideas of traditional Christianity. The task is one which many have of late years taken in hand both in Germany and in England, and there is probably little in these pages which is not derived from, or at least suggested by, the thoughts of others. The book may perhaps be found to differ from some of the more familiar English works of the same type by a franker admission of the necessity for theological reconstruction, while I have endeavoured to avoid the opposite mistake of supposing that Religion is possible for reflecting minds without a Theology, or that "liberal" Theology means vague and indefinite Theology.

The title (chosen only for want of a better) is intended to suggest two things—that all Theology is the result of a development, and that the development of religious thought is not finished yet. Theology arises out of the attempt to set the facts of the moral and religious consciousness in their due relation to the facts of science and of history. It is the attempt to build up a theory of the universe from the religious point of view. Christian Theology is the result of thought or reflection upon the life and teaching of Jesus Christ, or what at any given time that life and that teaching were understood to be. Theology is not necessarily valueless or superfluous because it is the result of development: Christian doctrine is not necessarily untrue or without value because it is not explicitly contained in the actual teaching of Christ, or of those earliest Theologians whose writings are contained in the New Testament Canon. It is of the highest importance that we should understand and make the most of the rich inheritance of Christian thought which the Church has handed down to us. At the same time it is equally important that we should recognize that some things have been believed by Christians—possibly by the whole Church of some particular period—which are no longer believable by us. At times the necessity for giving up some element of traditional dogma arises from the change which has taken place in our view of the facts of Christian history: at other times the modern Christian may accept the same view of the facts, but may find it impossible to be satisfied with some explanation of the facts which sufficed to "vindicate the ways of God to man" for past generations. Thus we can no longer accept the theory of "verbal" or of "plenary" inspiration, because we have discovered that the facts about the Bible are not as they were supposed to be when the theory was constructed; on the other hand, those who believe equally with St. Anselm or with Luther that Jesus Christ died, and died "for" men, can no longer accept without reservation their explanations as to why there was this necessity for Christ's death, because men's ideas of what is intrinsically just and reasonable are different from what they were in the days of St. Anselm or of Luther. It is necessary, then, to admit that here and there there must be some "giving up" of accepted doctrines, that at some points the ever active process of doctrinal development has got on to wrong lines, and must make a new departure. But in such cases we shall find that we are very often simply going back to some earlier stage in the development of doctrine, though generally the old doctrine will be held with a difference. The view of inspiration, for instance, to which modern Theologians are coming round is far more like that of the early Fathers than it is like the view of seventeenth-century Protestantism. But still it is not the same: it is impossible that a critical age should think exactly like an uncritical one. And in the great majority of cases there need be no "giving up." The defects of the development may be corrected not by going back, but by going on—by a new and larger interpretation of the old formulæ. The development has simply to be carried further. A doctrine may sometimes strike the modern mind as narrow or one-sided or inadequate because in its ancient form it suggests ideas or theories or views of the universe which have been transcended, but which do not really affect its essential truth. Indeed, the new interpretation will often discover a fuller and higher meaning into the old words than the traditional interpretation. Many theories of Inspiration, for instance, become erroneous only when what is asserted of the Bible or of the primitive Church is denied of other books or of the Church in modern times. It is impossible that men's theological ideas should not be continually affected by the changes which Philosophy and Science and historical criticism have produced in their ideas about other things. The process of reconstruction through which Theology is now visibly passing, even in the hands of those to whom the idea of theological innovation is least welcome, involves no greater revolution than has already occurred more than once in the Church's progressive attempt to understand and to formulate the relation of the "faith once delivered to the saints" to the continuous self-revelation of God to the human spirit.

For some readers I might perhaps illustrate what I mean by comparing the traditional dogmatic systems to the great masterpieces of ancient Philosophy. It is still possible for a student of

Philosophy to be a very faithful Platonist or Aristotelian, but it is impossible for any man acquainted with the methods and results of modern Science and historical criticism really to believe in all points as Plato or Aristotle believed. The most enthusiastic disciple must needs reject much of their Astronomy, their Cosmology, and their Physiology, and this difference between their way of looking at the universe and ours will necessarily affect the interpretation that is given to nearly every part of their strictly philosophical systems. And yet this difference may not diminish, it may even emphasize, the value of the essential elements in those Philosophies. For the modern Platonist is not less idealist than Plato, but more idealist, because he has got rid of certain ideas about a residual and unintelligible element in things which stood in the way of the full development of Plato's own system. In the same way may we not appropriate to ourselves many essential ideas of Athanasius or Thomas Aquinas without seeking to disguise the fact that we can never think about God or about Christ exactly as men thought in the fourth century or the thirteenth? Because the Christian thought of the future must be different in many ways from the thought of the past, it need not be less Christian. The Christian thought of the future should be more Christian than the thought of the past, just because we are getting to understand better than past generations the essential and eternal value of that life and that teaching on which all Christian doctrine is a commentary. That the Christianity of the future, while it finds ever fresh meanings in the teaching of its Founder, will never really go beyond what in germ and in essence is to be found in the religious consciousness of Christ, I have endeavoured to show in the Sermons on "the Historic Christ" and "the Unique Son."

It need hardly be said that it is only in the most fragmentary and imperfect way that that restatement or reinterpretation of Christian doctrine which is so much needed by the Church of our day could be attempted in such a work as the present, even by a Theologian better qualified for the task than the present writer can pretend to be. But even in the most inadequate of such attempts it is hardly possible—at least for a University preacher who happens to be a teacher of Philosophy—to avoid touching upon some of the difficulties which current Philosophies offer, or are supposed to offer, to Christian belief. It is my strong conviction that a Theology which is to satisfy thoughtful men in these days must rest upon a basis of thorough-going Metaphysic; and therefore I do not apologise for occasionally becoming a little metaphysical. At the same time I hope that even the more metaphysical of these discourses (chiefly the first and the last) may not be unintelligible to readers little versed in technical Philosophy; while I must ask philosophical readers (if such I should have) to bear in mind that these are *bonâ fide* sermons, that they were not originally intended to form a series, and that it is impossible, even in a University pulpit, to deal with the philosophical aspects of theological questions in a way which will satisfy philosophical experts. Even the more purely theological topics can of course be treated only in a very inadequate way. I have throughout endeavoured to keep in view the practical objects of which the preacher should never lose sight, and some of the sermons deal with wholly practical questions. The most that I can hope for is to help a few minds puzzled by the intellectual difficulties of our time to a more rational Christian faith.

The sermons were preached at different times in the course of the last ten years. I have, of course, printed nothing which I do not now believe, but I have not thought it necessary to consider how far in point of emphasis or of expression some of the earlier sermons would be different, were I now to rewrite them. I believe that, taken together, the sermons represent a consistent point of view, but I should be sorry to think that I had learned nothing in ten years.

Most of the sermons were preached as University Sermons at Oxford, either on the nomination of the Vice-Chancellor or as Select Preacher in 1895-1897.

One of them is a Cambridge University Sermon; two were preached at Aberdeen, and two in Balliol Chapel when I was for a short time Chaplain of that College. One sermon has previously been printed in the *Expositor*, one in the *Durham University Journal*, and others in the *Oxford Magazine*.

I have to thank several friends for their kind help in the revision of the proof-sheets, especially the Rev. Archibald Robertson, D.D., Principal of King's College, London.

H. RASHDALL

NEW COLLEGE, *April 18th*, 1898.

CONTENTS

                                                        PAGE

I. SPIRITUAL THEISM 1
  Preached before the University of Oxford,
  at St. Mary's, 1896.

II. THE HOLY TRINITY 21
  Preached in Balliol College Chapel,
  Trinity Sunday, 1894.

III. LIMITATIONS OF KNOWLEDGE IN CHRIST . . 33
  Preached before the University of Cambridge,
  December 23rd, 1889.

IV. THE HISTORICAL VALUE OF THE GOSPELS . 58
  Preached before the University of Oxford,
  at St. Mary's, 1895.

V. THE UNIQUE SON 77
  Preached in Balliol College Chapel, 1894.

VI. THE HISTORIC CHRIST 89
  Preached before the University of Oxford,
  at St. Mary's, 1896.

VII. REVELATION BY CHARACTER . . . 110
  Preached before the University of Oxford,
  at St. Mary's, 1894.

VIII. THE ABELARDIAN DOCTRINE OF THE ATONEMENT 128
  Preached before the University of Oxford,
  at St. Mary's, 1892.

CONTENTS

	PAGE
IX. JUSTIFICATION	146

   Preached before the University of Oxford,
     at St. Mary's, 1895.

X. THE IDEA OF SACRIFICE 164

   Preached in the University Chapel, Aberdeen,
     January 16th, 1898.

XI. THE RESURRECTION AND IMMORTALITY . 177

   Preached before the University of Oxford,
     at St. Mary's, 1897.

XII. THE CHRISTIAN DOCTRINE OF PROPERTY . 190

   Assize Sermon, preached before the University of Oxford,
     at St. Mary's, November 19th, 1893.

XIII. DIFFERENCES OF VOCATION . . . 210

   Preached before the University of Oxford,
     at St. Mary's, 1891.

XIV. CHRIST AND CULTURE 229

   Preached before the University of Oxford,
     at St. Mary's, 1897.

XV. THE IDEA OF THE CHURCH . . . 247

   Preached before the University of Oxford,
     at St. Mary's, 1897.

XVI. PERSONALITY IN GOD AND MAN . . 268

   Myrtle Lecture in the University of Aberdeen,
     February 16th, 1898.

I.

SPIRITUAL THEISM

Preached before the University of Oxford, at St. Mary's, 1896.

"God is a Spirit: and they that worship him must worship him in spirit and in truth."—JOHN iv. 24.

"GOD is a Spirit." We must turn for a moment to the context of these words if we are to appreciate their full depth of meaning and the originality of the teaching which they convey. The words occur, you will remember, in the conversation with the woman of Samaria; they are part of our Lord's reply to her question as to whether Jerusalem or Gerizim was the true place in which to worship God. The enquiry betrays what we may call the essence of Paganism. Amid the infinite variety of types assumed by polytheistic deities, this one feature is, I suppose, absolutely universal. The gods of Polytheism were essentially local deities. Their power was limited to such and such a spring, such and such a surrounding territory, such and such a nation, such and such an element or province of nature. The gods of the hills were not the same as the gods of the valleys. Originally, indeed, the

B

deity could only be approached at such and such an arbitrarily selected spot. The earliest symbols of deity were not statues, not representations of a god in human form, but simply stones or pillars at which the god was supposed to come into an almost physical contact with his worshippers.*

At first it is difficult to say how far the god was distinguished from the signs of his local presence. No doubt the crudest Theology ascribed some sort of spiritual being to the deity which inhabited the spring or the river, but still it was also true in a sense that the spring or the river was the god. As men's conception of their deities widened, the connexion between the god and the place of his special manifestation became less intimate. A slow process of what from the scientific point of view may be called evolution, but which may no less truly from the religious point of view be called Revelation, had gradually conducted the Jewish Nation to the belief that their national Deity, Jehovah, was the one and only God of all the earth. But even Monotheism by no means necessarily destroyed the belief in a special relation of God to a particular people and the land which it inhabited. To the Samaritan woman, as to her average Jewish contemporary, Jehovah was undoubtedly the only God; but He was a God who could be worshipped, if not indeed exclusively, yet with fullest and completest acceptance, only in Jerusalem or in Gerizim. That state of mind represented what we may call the last expiring

* Cf. ROBERTSON SMITH, *Religion of the Semites*, p. 84 *sq. et passim.*

stage of old-world Religion. In transcending this conception our Lord proclaimed the doom of Paganism. "The hour cometh and now is when the true worshippers shall worship Him in spirit and in truth," no matter whether in Jerusalem or elsewhere. It may be doubted whether up to that moment in the world's history this fundamental principle of Theism had ever been thus fully enunciated in complete freedom from all Jewish limitations. The teaching of Christ completes the long evolution of religious thought. It is well to emphasise this one particular aspect of Christ's work; this one fact that Jesus Christ was, so far as we know, the first teacher who taught Theism in complete freedom from Jewish limitations—that by itself is enough to place Him in an absolutely unique position in the history of religious thought. Strongly and rightly as we may feel that this fact does not exhaust the eternally unique significance of Jesus Christ for us, it is important that we should realize that He *has* this claim to our allegiance. Everyone who can sincerely join with Him in saying, "God is a Spirit, the only one, and He can be worshipped with equal acceptance everywhere if He be worshipped in a spiritual manner," proclaims himself by that confession to be in a very real sense a Christian. His Christianity—I am speaking, of course, of Christianity now simply from the point of view of theological opinion—his Christianity is no doubt imperfect; but he is not without a very good reason for calling himself a Christian. He does worship God, as Christ was the first to teach men to worship Him. Assuredly no other of the great historical religions can claim the allegiance of such a worshipper. For Mohammedanism, however grievously in other ways it has fallen back from the Christian standard, both of conduct and of creed, is in this matter not an independent religion, but an offshoot from the parent Judeo-Christian stock. So far, at least, the spiritual Monotheist is necessarily Christian; some meaning, at least, he must be able to ascribe to the unique position which Christian Theology has assigned to the Son of Man.

But it may be said: Granted that Judaism was the first great avowedly monotheistic Religion, and that Judaism culminates in Christianity, has not this truth of the Unity and Spirituality of God been more or less the underlying basis, at least of all Eastern religious thought? Are the gods of the Vedas anything more than so many manifestations of the One Spirit? And have not philosophers and philosophic poets, born in the bosom of Paganism both before and after Christ, reached, whether by philosophic argument or by spiritual intuition, the same precious truth? Were not the sages of Brahminism in an esoteric way—were not more explicitly Socrates, Plato, perhaps Sophocles, Monotheists at heart? Certainly we have no theological interest in attenuating the Theism to which all the greatest spirits of the world's history have, at least, approximated. If not before, yet very soon after Christ, Philosophy did, quite independently, teach a doctrine about God closely parallel to the teaching of our Lord. There is much truth and instructiveness (so far as it goes) in the point of view from which Christianity appears as the popular force which converted the esoteric teaching of the philosophers into a religion for the many;* and when we say Christianity in such a connexion we mean the historic personality of Christ.

> "Though truths in manhood darkly join,
> Deep-seated in our mystic frame,
> We yield all blessing to the name
> Of Him that made them current coin."

There would be nothing in that point of view which should diminish our sense of the uniqueness of Christ's position in the world's history, or even of the uniqueness of His nature. Yet after all, one can hardly recognise more than an approximation to the Christian doctrine of God in the teaching of any previous or even any later independent non-Christian thinker. The esoteric Monotheism of the East, and the speculative Theism of the Philosophers, are no doubt free from the local limitations of the ethnic religions: their conception of God is adequate enough in point of universality; but then it is usually more or less defective on the side of Personality. "God is a Spirit." It is more than doubtful whether even Plato, or any of the later philosophers who were unaffected by an indirect Christian influence, would have fully appreciated all that those simple words meant in the mouth of Jesus or of the simplest of His followers. From the point of the genuine Theist, the humblest Christian who had learned the true meaning of this teaching of the Master from St. John or St. Paul, even the least in that kingdom of God which Jesus had set up, saw more clearly into the heart of things

* See MARK PATTISON'S *University Sermons.*

than the greatest of Greek or Roman "Praeparatores Evangelii."

"God is a Spirit," if interpreted in the language of modern philosophy, amounts to this: "God is a Person." I want to try this afternoon briefly to emphasise this doctrine, and just to remind you of what is involved in it. Proof of it, in any sense in which proof can be offered, would involve too elaborate a philosophical argument for such an occasion as this. But perhaps a mere glance at some of the doctrines which it opposes may be the best way of bringing out at once its meaning and its reasonableness.

There is a whole school of modern Philosophy which, while using the name of God, repudiates the idea of personality. And some of the Theologians have, as it seems to me, prepared the way for those who desire to evacuate the name of God of all religious or ethical significance by insisting too unguardedly on the doctrine of God's infinity. What exactly was meant by infinity in the language of orthodox Theology I will not now enquire; but there certainly is a sense in which this doctrine of the infinity of God leads straight to conclusions from which every Christian thinker must recoil. That which is infinite, at least in one sense of the term, must exclude nothing. If there is anything which God is not, that by itself constitutes a limit. If God is to be strictly infinite, there can be nothing which He is not. I will not ask in what sense we can speak of the world as being not God. From the idealistic point of view the world may no doubt be regarded as the thought of God; and the thought of God is not outside Him. To say, therefore, that the world is not outside God is a statement which may be made without destroying His personality. But when we come to human souls the case is different. Certainly souls are not God. To say that they are part of God is to my mind a statement which is utterly and entirely without meaning, unless it is intended to imply that God is nothing but a collective name for the sum of individual minds. I know that I am not anybody else. We must not be led into the intricate and tangled controversy as to the nature of self-hood. But this much will, I think, commend itself to all minds except those constitutionally incapable of grasping the idea of personality—that the being "I" is inconsistent with being a *mere* part of anything whatever. There may be degrees of unity in consciousness. In certain diseased conditions the unity of self-consciousness may be indeed wholly broken up into two or more consciousnesses. But it is of the essence of self-hood to be a unity which excludes the idea of existing as a mere part of another thing or of another self. What I feel or think cannot actually be, though it may be like, what any other spirit feels or thinks. No other spirit, then, can be part of God. God is not you or I, or all of us together. That the soul is derived from God, made in the image of God, that it depends for its very being from moment to moment upon God, that the divine nature is more or less expressed in it, that it is capable of intimate union with God—all this Christian Theology has always asserted. If anyone likes to say that the soul is an emanation from God, that God is infused in a limited mode into the human organism, or reproduces Himself in the human soul, I do not know that there is any great objection to such language, if physical metaphors like these seem to anyone to make the matter clearer than the simple, orthodox statement that souls were created by God. But if God is not to be made a merely collective name, we are bound to hold that there is something which God is not. Some people will, perhaps, contend that this line of thought points to a pre-existent and uncreated origin of souls. Such an idea seems to me infinitely preferable to the pantheistic confusion between God and man; but for my own part I see no insuperable difficulties—except the difficulties which attend all attempts to think the relation between time and eternity—to the ordinary orthodox view that God limited Himself by the creation of souls. That seems to be quite as intelligible as the metaphors of emanation or infusion. But the point which I want to insist on now is simply this. If we admit that God is not any of the souls which owe their being to Him, then in the strict and philosophical sense of the word He is not infinite. Mr. Schiller, the author of the *Riddles of the Sphinx*, though few probably will be able to accept his system as a whole, deserves, to my mind, immense gratitude from all Christian Theologians for the logic and the boldness with which he has ventured to maintain the finitude of God. It is a question whether those who wish to preserve the idea of personality in God and man would not do well to follow his example. Once admit the infinity of God in what is, perhaps, the most ordinary philosophic sense of the word, and it follows that God can possess no personal consciousness; for it is of the essence of personality to distinguish oneself from other persons when once those other persons are in existence.

And what after all is rational consciousness without personality? Certainly there may be a consciousness below personality. We have reason to believe that the consciousness of the animals is of this nature, though even in the lowest animal consciousness there is something which excludes the idea of being included as part of a whole in another consciousness. To say that the most evanescent sensation of an amœba (if the amœba really possesses consciousness) is part of the consciousness of some other being is, as far as I can see, an absolutely unmeaning assertion. Another being might have a sensation like that of an amœba; in a sense he might even know all that the amœba feels and what it feels, though for us at least there is no way of knowing what others feel except through having ourselves felt something like it. But the fullest knowledge of what the amœba feels would not make its feeling pass over into the consciousness of the being that knew it. The feeling of the amœba must for ever* possess

---

* Here the Philosopher may object that whatever is real must be eternal or (as some would say) out of time. Kant's doctrine of the subjectivity of time is largely responsible for the tendency, firstly to deny reality to anything but the All, and then practically to resolve the All into a system of timeless relations. The best cure for the error of identifying the real with the timeless is to be found in Lotze's Chapter on Time in the *Metaphysics*. (Book II. chap. iii.)

a being of its own. If you like to say that this amounts to attributing a measure of personality to whatever has consciousness, I do not much care if it does. While it would be inconvenient to apply the term personality to any degree of unity in consciousness lower than that which is attained by the human soul, personality assuredly admits of degrees. Just as there may be degrees of personality below the human, just as there undoubtedly are degrees of personality in the human consciousness—Socrates was certainly more of a person than primitive man —so there may be degrees of personality much higher than the human. The difficulties of those who, while fully believing in the existence of a divine Mind, hesitate to attribute personality to Him, seem to me to arise from the assumption that personality implies not merely limitation but the precise limitations which we find in the human soul, whose knowledge comes to it piece by piece, advances to truth through error, and is at the highest but a partial knowledge of one small fragment of the universe. If you like to speak of a consciousness which is above personality there is no objection to doing so, provided (1) you make it quite clear that you do mean an actual consciousness not less distinct from other centres of consciousness than our own, and (2) that you do not, in getting rid of the term "person," get rid of the idea of will, which is an essential element in the highest idea of consciousness as we know it. To represent the divine consciousness as reason without will is to abstract from consciousness, as known to us, precisely the highest element in it, and then to hypostatise this perfectly unmeaning abstraction. Every act of thought as we know it implies an exercise of will as much as of reason. In the words of Mr. Bosanquet, "Whenever we are awake we are judging; whenever we are awake we are willing."* The will-less reason of some Hegelians is as unmeaning a phrase as an unconscious will of Schopenhauer.

There have been undoubtedly Philosophers who give a rather uncertain sound on this question of God's personality without meaning to deny Him a distinct self-consciousness. But with some of their followers and disciples the case is different. In the midst of the ambiguous phrases in which some writers of this School have enveloped their thought on this all-important subject, we may be really thankful to Mr. Bosanquet for having told us in plain language what he means. "While it appears to me," he tells us, "that nothing is gained for the interpretation of the world by the assumption of a divine intelligence underlying it, it also appears that beyond the abandonment of an otiose hypothesis nothing is determined in the interpretation of the world by surrendering this assumption."† He goes on to explain that while the world must undoubtedly be regarded as a machine, it is after all not at all a bad sort of machine. It is desirable for ethical purposes to assume that the machine is a good one, and therefore it is rational to make the assumption.

* *The Essentials of Logic*, p. 40.
† *The Permanent Meaning of the Argument from Design*, in *Proceedings of the Aristotelian Society* (1892), p. 44.

How it is possible still to contend that the world is rational, when Reason had nothing to do with the making or the guiding of it; how one can still be an Idealist when one has given up believing in a Mind for which and in which the world existed when human souls were not; how laws of nature (for that is all that Mr. Bosanquet really means by God) can without absolute materialism be supposed to exist *in* a material universe, or how (if they are not properties of a self-subsistent matter) they can exist in and for themselves; how again it is possible to take an optimistic view of a purely mechanical universe— these are problems which I will merely just commend to the attention of anyone who may have more or less entered upon that line of thought without fully appreciating its inherent tendencies. That Idealism, as understood by him, means pure Naturalism Mr. Bosanquet would be the first to admit; whether such Idealism is really Idealism any longer I must not now enquire.

But there is another way of looking at the matter which it will be instructive to notice. It is possible to deny personality to God without admitting the purely mechanical character of the universe. I must not attempt to reproduce the brilliant, however unsatisfying, argument by which another very distinguished Oxford Philosopher* attempts to show that neither matter as we know it, nor spirit as we know it, can be regarded as possessing in the fullest sense of the word reality. Knowledge, as we have it, he argues, implies a distinction between subject and

* Mr. F. H. BRADLEY, in *Appearance and Reality.* Ed. i. 1893.

object which cannot belong to the ultimate nature of things. All distinctions between subject and predicate, between self and not self, between mind and matter, between God and the world, are (we are told) overcome and transcended in the Absolute. Nothing is real except the whole. There is nothing very original or novel in Spinozism or Averroism such as this, though there is much that is original in the method by which it is reached. But this attempt to swallow up mind and matter in a reality which is neither, is scarcely ever really consistent. The human mind is very loath to commit intellectual suicide. It really has no choice but to conceive of the ultimate principle of things in terms of matter, or to conceive of it in terms of mind. And the distinguished writer to whom I am alluding, in spite of himself, is constantly betraying the fact that he really does think of the Absolute in terms of Mind. Unlike many so-called Idealists, unlike some who use far more spiritualistic, even more orthodox-sounding language, we possess in him a real and determined foe to Materialism. His own personal prejudice against everything that ordinary people understand by Religion, his avowed and savage hatred of Christianity, cannot destroy, though it may disguise, the value of the essential service which he has thus rendered to the Christian Faith. Once he even forgets himself so far as to attribute a character to the Absolute—a very unamiable character, it is true. The Absolute, it appears, possesses a sense of humour, and the existence of error in mankind is actually justified on the ground of the immense diversion which the spectacle of our blunders and absurdities may possibly afford to this same Absolute. Christians may indeed demur to a Philosopher attributing to his philosophic Divinity the truculent ferocity of a Moloch; but assuredly they cannot complain that this newest substitute for the God of Christendom is not a deity of a sufficiently anthropomorphic type.*

But now let me go on to notice what is the practical consequence of these metaphysical speculations as to the nature of God. To show you what is the consequence in a clear-sighted man of denying the Christian doctrine of God may perhaps be the best way of indicating its practical religious import.

"Most of those who insist on what they call 'the personality of God,'" says the writer whom I have just quoted, "are intellectually dishonest. They

---

* Lest I should be suspected of misrepresenting Mr. Bradley, I give the passage in full :—

"I confess that I shrink from using metaphors, since they never can suit wholly. The writer tenders them unsuspiciously as a possible help in a common difficulty. And so he subjects himself, perhaps, to the captious ill-will or sheer negligence of his reader. Still to those who will take it for what it is, I will offer a fiction. Suppose a collection of beings whose souls in the night walk about without their bodies, and so make new relations. On their return in the morning we may imagine that the possessors feel the benefit of this divorce; and we may therefore call it truth. But, if the wrong soul with its experience came back to the wrong body, that might typify error. On the other hand, perhaps the ruler of this collection of beings may perceive very well the nature of the collision. And it may even be that he provokes it. For how instructive and how amusing to observe in each case the conflict of sensation with imported and foreign experience. Perhaps no truth after all could be half so rich and half so true as the result of this wild discord—to one who sees from the centre." (*Ib.* p. 194.)

desire one conclusion, and, to reach it, they argue for another. But the second, if proved, is quite different, and serves their purpose only because they obscure it and confound it with the first. And it is by their practical purpose that the result may here be judged. This Deity, which they want, is of course finite, a person much like themselves, with thoughts and feelings limited and mutable in the process of time. They desire a person in the sense of a self, amongst and over against other selves, moved by personal relations and feelings towards these others—feelings and relations which are altered by the conduct of the others."*

Now a great part of this account may be accepted without scruple. Our author has nothing to say against it except that it is of course absurd, and that it is beneath him to discuss the matter with anyone who can hold it—with such a man for instance as Lotze, we may suppose. But it may be well to point out the ingenious way in which our great *malleus theologorum* has contrived to mix up a perfectly sound and reasonable doctrine which all Christians hold with one which they would indignantly repudiate.

In the first place we may protest altogether against the attempt to get rid of Theism by merely throwing in our teeth the difficulties created by the relation of Time to Eternity. In a sense no doubt God must be conceived of as above, if not out of time: so much Theologians have generally taught,

* *Appearance and Reality*, p. 532.

though (if they are wise) they go on to admit that to the idea of timeless or (better) of super-temporal existence we can attach no definite meaning. It is safest to content ourselves with saying that God's relation to the time-process cannot be the same as our relation to it. In any case, the difficulties presented by the relation of a timeless God to a series of events in time are no greater on our view of God's nature than are the relations of the Absolute to finite realities, or parts or aspects of Reality, upon our critic's view of the nature of the Absolute.

Secondly, a word as to the mutability of God. I see no reason why a Theist should not cordially accept the position, "The Deity is finite (in our author's sense), a self, amongst and over against other selves." And that relation of other selves to God can only be envisaged after the analogy of the relation between two human selves. It must be represented so, or we must do without any idea whatever of a spiritual relation between God and the ultimate principle of things, which not even our critic is willing to do, for he is very anxious to be reconciled with his Absolute. If we are to represent God as occupying any spiritual relation towards man, we cannot help representing this attitude towards us as dependent upon the varying thoughts, feelings, and actions of our souls. And these thoughts, feelings, and actions are admittedly in time. But, to say nothing of modern Theologians, the old Hebrew Prophets, to whom we so largely owe this precious doctrine of the personality of God, were quite aware that such language must not be understood to imply real changes of purpose in God. "I am the Lord, I change not." All the successive events of the world's history must be regarded as so many expressions of a single Will or Purpose or Character, a character which in the New Testament is represented to us as a consistent and changeless Love.*

The wrath of God against sin is as changeless as His Love, of which indeed it is but one side or aspect. To represent God as "moved by personal relations and feelings towards other selves—feelings and relations which are altered by the conduct of the others" may be a very inadequate representation of the real nature of God; but at least we feel sure that it expresses more of the truth than any attempt to get at the nature of God by eliminating from our conception of Him all that involves relation to other selves. We think of God best by likening Him to what is highest within our knowledge. To deprive God of personality, to deprive Him of relation to others, is to deprive Him both of knowledge and of love. For the clearness with which he has demonstrated the inevitable tendency of a line of thought, which has often attracted even Christian minds, we cannot be too grateful to the distinguished thinker whom I have ventured to criticise.

And perhaps we ought to be thankful also if these unfriendly criticisms should lead us to ask more

* When we attempt to represent to ourselves this Will, we necessarily conceive of Him as a Being persisting throughout a succession of changing states, states which vary as our attitude towards Him varies. That representation no doubt falls short of the reality—how far, in what way, we do not know. That perhaps we could only know by getting out of our own relation to time and into God's.

C

seriously than we are apt to do whether the idea of worship sometimes avowed by Christians does not at times lay itself open to such caricatures as that which I have quoted to you.

In the words of our text the truth about God is made the basis of a truth about worship. Because God is a Spirit, those who worship Him must worship Him in spirit and in truth. Our worship must be worthy of our conception of God's nature. Our worship must not be such worship as is implied by the idea that a prayer would be effectual in Jerusalem which would have been offered in vain at Gerizim—valid if offered in this form, by this official, in this church, invalid if offered otherwise. Worship must consist in the effort of the human spirit to identify itself with the Divine—not in mystical, self-destroying unity, but in the direction of its desires, its aspirations, its will. Formal worship, public or private, can be only a means to bringing about this conformity of the will, and therefore of the life, to God's Will. Simple as this principle is, admitted as it is in form by Theologians of every school, it is often forgotten, as it seems to me, in the common objections to prayer and worship, and not sufficiently remembered in the common apologies for them. In worship we are not seeking to effect a change in the Will of God. In that sense indeed we do repel the charge that we treat God as mutable. We seek to change only our disposition towards Him, and to bring our souls into a state of conformity with His Will. Upon the state of our souls and our wills depends the character of our lives, and the course of events in the world outside us. Prayer, therefore, *must* be effectual. It is matter of experience that such deliberate efforts, on the part of individuals and of societies, do powerfully assist in bringing the will in conformity with the All-perfect Will. It is one great organ or channel or occasion, if we cannot venture to say that it is the only occasion, of God's self-revelation to the individual soul. Worship, therefore, is necessary. Its form may change, but some form of it is an eternal demand of the human soul.

And once again the worship of a God who is a Spirit must be in truth. Our worship must conform to our best intellectual conceptions about God and His Will. We have reason to believe, for instance (though I for one cannot recognise any necessity of thought for believing), that God works by general laws.* We ought not, therefore, to seek—it is better,

---

* This does not exclude the possibility of abnormal or even unique events, due to abnormal or even unique results of law, known or unknown. The truth is, we know too little of the relations of mind and organism to draw a sharp line between the natural and the supernatural in this sphere. Recorded instances of abnormal control by mind over the processes of physical nature must be accepted or rejected in accordance with the evidence, but the evidence required to establish them is less or greater according to the degree of their departure from the known analogies of nature. I believe that those commonly called miracles, which are of most religious importance—the general fact that Christ cured disease by spiritual influence and the Resurrection Vision—are precisely those for which well-established analogies are strongest. Given an exceptional personality, there is no reason against the belief that His power over nature may have been exceptional also; but such a power need not necessarily "violate the laws of nature" if the ordinary facts of volitional activity do not violate them. The treatment of the miraculous element in the Christian history with which I feel most in sympathy is that of Mr. Frederick Myers' most suggestive criticism on Renan in his *Modern Essays*.

as far as we can, to avoid language which implies that we seek—to change that course of nature in the physical universe, or even to ask God to work miracles in the moral universe. If we were a little bolder in proclaiming distinctly what worship is not, we should, perhaps, find men more willing to appreciate what it really is, and to make the sacrifice of time and ease and inclination which is demanded by this great task—the training of our wills in association with our brethren for the doing of God's Will in the inner and the outer life.

II.

THE HOLY TRINITY

Preached in Balliol College Chapel, Trinity Sunday, 1894.

"He shall take of mine, and shall shew it unto you."
JOHN xvi. 15.

"THE Holy Ghost is the love wherewith the Father loves the Son and the Son the Father."* Such is the teaching of St. Augustine,

---

* The Holy Spirit is shown to be "quo genitus a genitante diligatur genitoremque suum diligat."—*De Trin.*, vi. 5. (Cf. *De Fide et symbolo*, 19, 20, and *De Civ. Dei*, xi., c. 26, where the parallel between the Divine Trinity and the human mind is insisted on : "Nam et sumus et nos esse novimus et id esse et nosse diligimus.") St. Augustine is, no doubt, anxious to show that in God "dilectio" is a "substantia," because in God there is no distinction between substance and accident. This is, of course, a realistic technicality to which it is difficult for the modern mind to attach much meaning, though, no doubt, parallels might be found in modern metaphysicians. To understand the scholastic doctrine of the Trinity it is further necessary to remember that the love of the Father for the Son is really the love of God for the objects of His own thought, *i.e.*, for His creatures. "Verbum igitur in mente conceptum est repræsentativum omnis ejus quod actu intelligitur. Unde in nobis sunt diversa verba, secundum diversa quæ intelligimus. Sed quia Deus uno actu et se et omnia intelligit, unicum Verbum ejus est expressivum non solum Patris, sed etiam creaturarum." (*Summa Theol.*, Pt. I. Q. xxxiv. Art. 3.) When, therefore, some modern Divines talk about an intercourse or society subsisting between the Father and the Son, meaning by the Son a conscious being, distinct alike from God, the world, and the "assumptus homo," Jesus Christ, they are and the doctrine is repeated by the great schoolmen in a more general form: " The love by which we love

using language which an orthodox scholastic Theologian would probably have pronounced to be sheer Tritheism. It is true that the Scholastics speak of a "relatio" between the Persons of the Holy Trinity (*i.e.*, a relation between the Power of God, the Wisdom of God, and His Love or Will), but they do not forget that "relatio in Deo sit idem quod sua essentia." Anyone who thinks that the doctrine here maintained is Sabellianism should read Pt. I. Q. xxviii. of the *Summa*. Stripped of technicalities, the Catholic doctrine differs from Sabellianism inasmuch as it asserts (i.) that these different activities are essential to God's nature, not appearances or modes which can be put on or off, and (ii.) that the Incarnation implies an indwelling of the Sapientia Dei in a human soul, but not that Christ was simply God (the whole Trinity) in a human body—carrying with it (as the Patripassians held) the consequence that the Father died upon the cross. All the difficulties of the doctrine of the Trinity have arisen from thinking of that relation between God and the pre-existing Logos as if it were of exactly the same kind as the relation between God and the Incarnate Son. Of course (if we like to eliminate the element of time) we may think of God as having an eternal relation to the man Jesus Christ even before his actual birth, and the idea of the pre-existence of Christ (not merely the Logos) in the form in which it appears in the New Testament seems to have arisen out of the strong conviction that the coming of the Messiah was part of the eternal counsel of God—the central event of the world-plan as it existed in the mind of God. For an admirable discussion of this question see BEYSCHLAG, *New Test. Theology* (E. T., 1895), I. p. 249 *sq.*, II. p. 79 *sq.*

The doctrine of the Trinity, thus understood, is not a mere scholastic subtlety. It asserts just the essence of Christian Theism, *i.e.*, that God is not mere Power or mere Thought or mere Love, but the three combined. It is not surprising to find a learned and candid Unitarian Divine acknowledging that "there were certain elements in Christian experience which, when taken up and interpreted by Greek philosophy, necessarily resulted in this doctrine; and though we may believe that the form and the terminology of the doctrine were derived from a foreign source, we may nevertheless admit the reality of fundamental Christian facts which imparted to it all its religious vitality." (DRUMMOND, *Via, Veritas, Vita*, p. 203.) In the passage which follows Dr. Drummond seems to state the heart of the Trinitarian doctrine, though I do not, of course, mean to assent to

THE HOLY TRINITY

God and our neighbour is the Holy Ghost," * they say. These *dicta* are, I think, by themselves enough to show you that when the Fathers or the Schoolmen spoke of a Trinity of Persons in the Unity of the Godhead, they used the word "Person" in a sense very different from its usual modern acceptation. It would be meaningless to call the love of one being for another a person in our modern sense of the word. Thomas Aquinas explains the terms "Persona" by "Proprietas": he speaks indifferently of "tres Personae" or "tres proprietates." By "proprietates" we may, perhaps, understand three distinct and essential properties or powers or activities or modes of existence.

But I will not lead you any further into the mazes of the Scholastic Theology. I only want just to point out what I do think requires at the present day to be stated in the plainest and most unmistakable language, that those who framed what are still the accepted orthodox formulæ on this great subject did not mean by Person what nine-tenths of those who have to-day repeated the Athanasian Creed naturally enough suppose it to mean. I am afraid that most people—at least in their orthodox moments, when they are trying to realize to themselves the doctrine of the Holy Trinity—think of the three Persons as three distinct beings, three consciousnesses, three minds,

---

everything in his book. Catholic doctrine does not become Unitarianism because it is implicitly or explicitly held by some who call themselves Unitarians.

* PETRUS LOMBARDUS, *Sententiae*, Lib. I., i., Dist. XVII. So St. THOMAS AQUINAS, *Summa Theol.*, Pt. I., Q. xxxvii.

three wills. Nothing less than that could be implied if by Person were meant anything like what is meant by it in ordinary discourse. I trust I have said enough to show that, whatever be the exact shade of meaning which this highly technical expression bore to those who first introduced it, it certainly did not mean that. And when this admission is made, it further becomes evident that if the doctrine of the Holy Trinity is to have any real meaning or importance to us at the present day, it is much in need of a little translation into the language and thought of the present day.

Technicalities apart, the essence of the doctrine of the Holy Trinity is surely this—that God reveals Himself, that it is His nature eternally to reveal Himself. His revelation of Himself did not begin with the coming of Christ. Creation is itself in a sense a revelation of God, an embodiment of His thought. "All things were made," says St. John, "through or by means of the Word or Reason of God." In a much higher sense God was revealed in the growing intellect and conscience of mankind: "In Him was life, and the life was the light of men." In all the long course of moral and intellectual development which preceded the coming of Christ the eternal Word of God was communicating or revealing God to man, most clearly and fully no doubt (in the moral and spiritual sphere) to the later Jewish prophets, but (as the greatest of the Christian Fathers always recognised) not by any means to them alone. Yet all previous revelations of God were but broken and imperfect revelations.

The Revelation had been made, as the author of the Epistle to the Hebrews puts it, πολυμερῶς καὶ πολυτρόπως—"in divers portions and in divers manners"—till in the end of these days God spake to man by His Son.* In the life and teaching and character of Christ the mind, the will, the character of God was revealed as it had never been revealed before. And in one sense that revelation was final. But it wanted to be brought home to the minds and consciences of man; it wanted to be continually applied to the changing needs and aspirations of each successive age. And, when we say that we believe in the Holy Spirit, we say that we believe that God is still revealing Himself; that God is still in contact with the human spirit; that God is still making Himself known in the great movements of action and of thought, of history and of literature, and in the secret depths of individual souls.

There will always, no doubt, to the Christian consciousness be an essential difference between the revelations which preceded and those which follow the coming of Christ. For the Christian consciousness all that can be revealed to man now, in the strictly moral and religious sphere, can be only a development—a bringing out of what is latent in the teaching and character of Christ. It is but a taking of Christ's, and a showing unto us. Every improvement that has taken place, whether in the acknowledged moral standard or in the operative ideal of successive ages, seems to us so plainly written in the teaching of Christ, that each age

* Hebrews i. 1.

marvels how men can ever have called themselves Christians and yet not have seen it there. The Revelation made in Christ is inexhaustible; but there were many things which the world to which Christ came could not hear or see in it then. It is only the continued working of God's Spirit in the souls of men that could bring to men's remembrance all that the historic Christ implicity had said. The Christian Revelation was final, just because it contained in itself the germ of all future development; just because it possessed, and still possesses, the capacity of taking up into itself, and transforming and harmonising, all that is permanent and essential in other revelations.

God is Power, and God is Wisdom, and God is Will—that is the recognised scholastic explanation of the doctrine of the Holy Trinity. Or, since the Will of God is always a loving Will, the Schoolmen tell us the Holy Spirit may indifferently be spoken of as Will or as Love; from the union of Power and Wisdom in God's nature there proceeds a loving Will.

God is Power and Wisdom and Love. God is revealed fully and perfectly in Christ. God is revealing Himself ever more and more perfectly in the souls of men. That is the sum and substance of the doctrine of the Holy Trinity as defined by the most unimpeachable exponents of orthodox Theology. And if there are other parts of the technical formulæ on this subject which we find strange, or arbitrary, or unintelligible, let us solace ourselves with the avowal of the really great Old Catholic Theologian, Dr. Döllinger :—

THE HOLY TRINITY

"Few people here" (he says in reply to the question whether he attached the same extreme importance which some people do in England to the Athanasian Creed)—"few people here would insist on rigid agreement with formulas in a matter of such inscrutable mystery as the Trinity. In some particulars it is impossible to know the meaning of the terms used. The most subtle philosopher and the most profound Theologian cannot explain the difference between 'generation' and 'procession' in the 'generation of the Son' and the 'procession of the Spirit.'"*

The doctrine of the Holy Trinity is not an unpractical doctrine without meaning or importance for us at the present day. It brings before us in close connexion the two great aspects of the divine self-revelation. It is, as it seems to me, of almost equal practical importance that we should try to appreciate and appropriate to ourselves all that God once said to the world by His Son, and that we should not close our ears to what the Spirit is saying to the Churches in our own day. It is of almost equal importance for the illumination of our own souls and the guidance of our own lives, that we should seek to realize and to keep ever present to our minds a true and living image of the historic

---

* "Recollections of Dr. Döllinger," by ALFRED PLUMMER, D.D., in *Expositor*, Ser. iv., vol. i. (1890), pp. 425, 426. By Aquinas, *Summa Theol.*, Pt. I., Q. xxvii., the "generatio" of the Word is actually spoken of as a "processio," and in the Sentences of Peter the Lombard (Lib. I., Dist. xiii.) there is a section showing "quod non potest distingui a nobis inter generationem Filii et processionem Spiritus Sancti."

Son of God, and that we should recognise as a revelation of the Spirit of God all that is true and noble in the thoughts and ideas and spiritual achievements of other ages, and not least of our own.

The fact is, it is impossible to understand what that great historic revelation of God in Christ means to us, except in the light of the continuous revelation of the Spirit. The historic revelation can never mean to us exactly what it meant to any former age; no two ages in the past have ever interpreted it exactly alike. There is a danger lest it should cease to mean anything at all to us, unless we do constantly seek to reinterpret it to ourselves in the light of present-day knowledge and experience. And is it superfluous to remind ourselves that to do this demands, on our part, a little effort and a little trouble? It does require an effort to understand what Christianity means to us at the present day. It demands effort of other kinds—effort in prayer and effort in life: the effort to will and to do the truth that we possess. But, all-important as the moral effort is, to understand Christianity demands also intellectual effort. It does require a good deal of effort, I know, side by side with studies which may seem to have very little relation to such matters, to undertake however little reading of a theological or religious kind. And yet if we take a sufficiently large and liberal view of what is meant by Theology, Theology ought not merely to be looked upon as a merely professional study, as a specialism with which a well-educated Christian man can afford to be wholly unacquainted. By

Theology we mean the intellectual appreciation of religious truth in its relation to other branches of knowledge. Knowledge progresses; and Theology must progress with it, or become a mere fossil Science. Theology must be progressive, both in the world at large and in each individual mind. No two ages at different levels of intellectual development can ever think exactly alike about Religion. Nor can the religious ideas of the man be exactly those of the child. Now in this place our knowledge, our ideas on all other subjects are, or ought to be, growing and expanding. Can we reasonably expect that our Religion should retain the place it ought to have in our thoughts and in our lives if we do nothing to add to our faith knowledge? Sooner or later we must come to outlive the Theology of the nursery. Are we doing anything to fill its place?

> " Duly, daily, needs provision be
> For keeping the soul's prowess possible,
> Building new barriers as the old decay,
> Saving us from evasion of life's proof,
> Putting the question ever 'Does God love,
> And will ye hold that truth against the world.'"*

For those who have little leisure for such studies, and who have no intention of becoming Theologians, it is not always, of course, the more technical kind of theological writing that will be found most stimulating; though one may perhaps be allowed to regret that a knowledge of the elementary facts about New

* BROWNING, *A Death in the Desert.*

Testament criticism, as much knowledge (say) as an average classical student thinks it necessary to possess about the Homeric question, should not be more common than it is even among highly cultivated men. I believe that a little such knowledge is a very real help even to the spiritual comprehension of the New Testament. But even for the fruitful understanding of the New Testament some of us have found such a book as *Ecce Homo*, or some more modern work on the life and teaching of Christ, of more help than many commentaries. And some of the best Theology of the day must be sought for in books which would not usually be called Theology at all. The living and moving ideas of those who have most powerfully and fruitfully influenced the religious thought of our own time, or at least of the generation just gone by—the ideas of men like Maurice and Kingsley, of Frederick Robertson and Arnold—may be gathered from their Biographies almost better than from their writings.

There is Theology in Kingsley's novels and Newman's poetry, as well as in their sermons. It is no vague or emasculate Theology, again, that has found expression in the poetry of Tennyson and of Browning. But if our belief in the Holy Spirit is to be a really vital belief, if it is to correspond with the facts of history and the experience of life, we must recognise that the Spirit of God has spoken much in these latter days through voices which are not professedly Christian at all. Those who believe that Jesus Christ is in a unique sense *the* Son of God—the brightness of his Father's glory and the express image of his

Person—must no doubt regard the ideal embodied in him as the norm or criterion by which to test all other theories of conduct, all ideals of life, all schemes of social regeneration. By that canon we shall try the Spirits, whether they be of God. But prophets cannot be divided into true and false so easily as we are apt to imagine was the case in days gone by. We cannot help recognising that God has had something to say to this generation, as to other generations, by the mouth of people whose thoughts and whose characters were not wholly conformed to the mind of Christ. To many Carlyle has no doubt proved a true prophet of God, in spite of his essentially pagan hero-worship and his loveless temper. Everyone recognises the high Christian teaching in the novels of George Eliot, if we may occasionally feel in her writings the void background of Materialism. Again, at the present day we often see the social side, at least, of Christian Ethics both preached and practised by men whose religious views we may detest, and whose social schemes we may distrust, with an earnestness and a self-denial which have often been lacking within the pale of formal Christianity. It is by strange methods and strange voices that the Christian Church has sometimes been led to the understanding of her own creed. The Spirit bloweth where it listeth. The Spirit of God moves not only upon the sails of the Church's ship, but also upon the chaotic waters of human life around. The Spirit takes of Christ's and shows it unto men by other organs than by that of his Church. It is the Church's mission ultimately to absorb into herself and to make her own all that the Spirit shall teach by whatever organ He may speak.

And what is the Church's mission collectively is really in its measure the task of each one of us as a member of that Church. Each one of us has to build up for the illuminating of his own individual soul, and then to live out, what is really a Theology. A man's Theology is his theory of the universe. And our ideal of life ought surely to rest upon a theory of some kind—vague and dim and inarticulate as it must needs be for many in these days. The man without a Theology is in danger of becoming a man without an ideal.

III.

LIMITATIONS OF KNOWLEDGE IN CHRIST.*

Preached before the University of Cambridge, December 23rd, 1889.

"Have this mind in you, which was also in Christ Jesus: who, being in the form of God, counted it not a prize to be on an equality with God, but emptied himself, taking the form of a servant, being made in the likeness of men."—PHILIPPIANS ii. 5, 6. (R.V.)

IN these verses an aspect of our Lord's Incarnation is brought before us, which it is, if I mistake not, of especial importance to insist upon at the present day. It is a well-recognised fact that in the early Church as many heresies arose from an unwillingness

---

* Since this Sermon was written the question has been brought into prominence by Canon Gore in *Lux Mundi* (1889), in his Bampton Lectures, *The Incarnation of the Son of God* (1891); and in the learned *Dissertations on subjects connected with the Incarnation* (1895). The Bishop of Manchester has also dealt with the subject in the *Teaching of Christ* (1891)—a little book which contains more of the best results of modern theological thought and investigation in a smaller compass than any book with which I am acquainted. Had these works already appeared, I might have spoken less apologetically, though (as will be seen from the Sermon) I hold that in certain directions the theory of limitation in our Lord's knowledge must be carried further than Canon Gore would admit.

to admit the reality of our Lord's human nature as from unwillingness to admit the reality of his Godhead. At the present day Christians rightly regard the Divinity of Christ as the very core and centre of the Christian Faith; and the jealousy with which we habitually guard this fundamental doctrine, the suspicion with which we view any uncertainty of utterance or laxity of statement thereupon, the knowledge that it is just at this point that the great gulf is fixed between those who regard Christianity as a divine revelation adapted to the wants of all nations and of all time, and those who look upon it as merely one of the many forms in which the religious idea has from time to time historically embodied itself—all these causes have combined to make us somewhat afraid of insisting upon the complementary truth of the real humanity. Even in those parts of the New Testament Canon whose Christology is least explicit, Jesus is habitually spoken of in a way quite inconsistent with a belief, on the part of the writers, that he was a *mere* man. But, side by side with the passages which accord to Christ an exceptional nature and position, we meet with expressions and modes of speech which many a modern preacher would hesitate to use without qualification or explanation. A modern preacher or writer who should speak of our Lord (as he spoke of Himself) as one among the prophets, or who should employ some nineteenth century equivalent for St. Peter's phrase, "Jesus, a *man* approved of God," without balancing his statement by some higher theological formula, would be in some danger of losing his reputation for orthodoxy. Still more apparent is this caution or timidity about emphasising the human side of our Lord's nature when we examine the inferences which are drawn by popular Theology from the fact of our Lord's Divinity and the explanations which are given in orthodox commentaries of those passages of the Gospels or the Epistles in which limitations to our Lord's power or knowledge seemed to be hinted at. At the present day we no longer, indeed, find that difficulty in admitting the reality of our Lord's *sufferings* which lay at the root of Gnosticism and so many early forms of heresy. The reality of our Lord's human body and of all those mental affections or passions which spring most directly from the conditions of the bodily organism—the reality of pain, of sorrow, of human affection, of loneliness, of bodily weakness and weariness in Jesus Christ—the reality of all these attributes of his human nature has been branded into the popular religious consciousness by their intimate connexion with the doctrine of the Atonement. On the *emotional* side our Lord's humanity is accepted without difficulty and without scruple. But in the current ideas about the *intellectual* part of our Lord's nature does not the notion of a human brain, a growing and expanding human intelligence, a human reason, tend very much to drop out of sight? Is there not, in short, a good deal of latent Apollinarianism in orthodox popular teaching upon this matter?

The proper corrective of such a one-sided view of our blessed Lord's nature seems to me to be to insist upon the Pauline doctrine of the κένωσις* or self-emptying of the Son, which is brought before us in these verses. "He emptied Himself." Of what did he empty Himself? The only clue which we have to St. Paul's thought on this matter is contained in the immediately preceding words, "Who, being in the form of God, thought it not a thing to be clutched at to be equal with God, *but* emptied Himself."

It is, indeed, difficult to say whether as a matter of pure exegesis we should hold that when the μορφὴ of the slave was assumed, the μορφὴ of God was temporarily laid aside, put (so to speak) into abeyance. But at all events we may fairly represent the thought of the passage by saying that when the Eternal Wisdom, the Eternal Thought, the Eternal Word of God was united with a human soul, some at least of the divine attributes—though not lost—ceased to be manifested in the man Christ Jesus. Of what attributes of Godhead then was the Incarnate Word divested? Certainly of the divine Omnipresence. That surely is implied in the very idea of Incarnation. The ubiquity of our Lord's Human Body or Human Nature has never (I believe) been entertained except as a support for the Lutheran doctrine of Consubstantiation. Hardly less certainly

---

* I do not mean to identify myself with any of the later technical theories usually known as "kenotic." Many of them seem either to imply an actual demission (so to speak) of Godhead which is unintelligible, or to imply that the Second Person of the Holy Trinity, prior to and independently of the Incarnation, is to be regarded as possessing knowledge and reason of His own distinct from that of the Father, a doctrine which is happily as unorthodox as it is irrational. (See above, Sermon ii.)

did the Incarnate Word empty Himself of the Divine Omnipotence. Omnipotence is not compatible with the form of a slave. I suppose that this will on reflection be admitted by everyone. Limitation surely is essential to the very idea of humanity. It is scarcely possible to assign any real meaning to the humanity of our Lord Jesus Christ if we do not recognise that by acceptance of our human nature the divine power and nature were defined, conditioned, limited. The miracles recorded in the Gospels do not prove Omnipotence, though they do prove the possession of more than the normal control of the human will over the processes of physical nature.

We must remember, moreover, that the miracles which are usually regarded as the most striking manifestations of Divine Power are more often ascribed directly to the Father than to the will of the Incarnate Son. "Him God raised up" appears to have been the earliest and most usual form of the apostolic proclamation.

Weiss, indeed, assumes as a universal principle that our Lord only worked miracles when he felt within Him that it was the Father's will to work them.* This seems to me much more than we can possibly know. But certainly Christ's works of healing would to some minds lose much of their naturalness—they would constitute a far less touching manifestation of tender, human affection than they do now, if we were forced to believe that in that human soul which felt sympathy with the sufferer,

* *Life of Christ* (E. T.), p. 195.

and felt the power to relieve his pain, there was also all the while the consciousness of capacity to bring to an end by one word of power all the sufferings of all humanity. Undoubtedly we are here touching upon the fringe of that one great insoluble enigma—the mystery of pain, the mystery of evil. But it is just because it does so much to facilitate the belief that the universe has its origin in, and is governed by an unseen Love, that the Godhead of Christ is so unspeakably precious to us; and I confess that the Love which the Incarnation proclaims to us would become to me less real a thing if I did not believe that in the assumption of our humanity there was a real self-emptying—not a continued voluntary non-exercise, but a real surrender—of divine power in (to use the technical language of Theology) the "man assumed."

"He emptied himself," then, of Omnipotence. Must we not also say of Omniscience? Here we confront one of the great *quæstiones vexatæ* of orthodox Theology. The great Greek Fathers, with their philosophical education, for the most part recognise the existence of ignorance in the human soul of Christ. Augustine and some other Latin Fathers unfortunately took the other side, and to save our Lord's omniscience practically impeached His veracity. In spite of the text, "Of that day and that hour knoweth no man, neither the Son nor the Father," they maintained that even as man He really did know, but thought it inexpedient to tell, the date of the Judgment. The question was still more explicitly discussed in the medieval Schools, especially in that golden age of medieval thought, the twelfth century. Although the authorities which have dominated the after course of dogmatic thought in both the Roman and the Anglican Churches have mostly decided that the Incarnate Son, even in his human consciousness, enjoyed the perfection of divine knowledge, it has generally been considered a perfectly orthodox opinion to maintain the contrary. But it is obvious that the difficulty was one which could not be felt in medieval times as it is felt to-day. In the Middle Ages the question was in the main one of mere speculative curiosity. That the Galilean carpenter, Jesus of Nazareth, should have possessed a mind stored with the answers to the questions of Physics and Metaphysics which were debated by the medieval doctors—this was, indeed, a supposition which postulated an enormous miracle: but miracle as such was no difficulty to the medieval mind, and the supposition was one which, in the then state of human knowledge, hardly involved any intrinsic contradiction or impossibility. When the Bible and the Sentences, Boethius and Aristotle, the Canon Law and the Civil Law, Hippocrates and Galen made up between them nearly all the ultimate sources of the secular knowledge that the human mind was thought capable of attaining, the *omne scibile* could hardly be said to lie beyond the reach of conceivable attainment for an extraordinarily gifted individual.* At least

---

* Albert the Great explicitly defends the Omniscience of the Mother of Christ by proving in detail that she must have known the *Trivium* and *Quadrivium*, the Science of Medicine, the Civil and Canon Law, the Bible and Sentences. (*Opera*, Lugduni, 1651, T. xx. p. 80.)

the difficulty was fairly met by adopting the distinction between implicit and explicit knowledge, and ascribing to the Incarnate Son at least an implicit Omniscience. But, now that all the books which can be read in the longest of human lives are but a thousandth or a millionth part of the books in which acquired knowledge is stored—now that the idea of finality in philosophical, or political, or scientific conceptions has been supplanted by the idea of indefinite progress—now that this enormously augmented mass of accumulated knowledge is felt to represent but a few pebbles picked up on the shores of an ocean of Truth, infinite and unexplored—in presence of this expanded view of the all which there is to know, the difficulty which the medieval thinker disposed of by a "distinctio" and a "convenienter" weighs with far more terrific force upon minds that would fain reconcile enlarged conceptions of the universe with the acceptance of an historical Christianity.

So long as we confine ourselves to the region of scientific knowledge there will, I imagine, be little difficulty in admitting that the knowledge possessed by the man Christ Jesus was limited. It is when we come to the region of religious knowledge, or (more properly speaking) to the points of contact between religious questions and questions of Science or History or literary criticism that the difficulty becomes most serious. I know that I am here approaching the region of impenetrable mystery. Mystery undoubtedly must be admitted to be inherent in any conception of a divine-human nature. Most of us, I imagine, would wish that some even of those questions of Christology, upon which the early Councils undertook to decide with legal rather than philosophical precision, had been allowed to remain open questions, however entirely we may feel that, if the questions must be raised and must be decided, the Catholic answer to them is the most logical one. Still more often repellent to the natural instinct alike of reverence and of good sense are some of the later scholastic definitions about the Holy Trinity and the Incarnation, however great their superiority in intellectual strength to the treatment which such questions receive in many of the books which do duty for treatises of dogmatic Theology among ourselves. An attitude of reverent agnosticism upon such questions is the attitude which will often commend itself to our minds as at once the safest and the most rational. But there seem to be very pressing reasons why this particular question of the knowledge of Jesus Christ should be raised, and why the kenotic view (as I believe it is called) of our Lord's Incarnation should be not merely admitted, but insisted upon and emphasised.

The difficulties that are felt about the evidence for miracles the moment the question is abstracted from the unique personality of Christ, the changes which have taken place in the views of all intelligent men about the inspiration of Scripture, and the application of the comparative method to the study of Religions, have all tended to give a greatly increased prominence to the words of our Lord Himself. The wisest of modern Apologists no longer attempt to prove our Lord's Divinity primarily by

His miraculous credentials. The tendency is rather to begin with an investigation of the *character* with which the Gospel-narrative presents us. The originality and the perfection of the character are regarded as evidence for the sincerity of the words. And then the words are examined with a view to showing that they could not with sincerity have been used by any mere man—by anyone who was not conscious of a more than human authority, of being in some absolutely unique and solitary union with the Almighty Father.

The evidence of Christ's consciousness is rightly coming among thoughtful Theologians to be looked upon as the unassailable rock upon which the belief in the divineness of the Person must ultimately repose. And this view is happily beginning, though only beginning, to find general expression in the more popular kinds of religious literature. But sometimes we find this mode of argument pushed to unwise lengths. It is rightly admitted, for instance, that the importance and authority of the Old Testament for us depend on its intimate connexion with the New. Our Lord testified to the inspiration of the Old Testament prophets. He regarded Himself as fulfilling the Messianic predictions. It is scarcely possible, therefore, to believe in the reality even of Christ's divine Mission, still less in His Divine Nature, and at the same time to regard the Messianic idea in the Old Testament as a mere fancy inspired by the irrepressible national vanity of a conquered people. So far there is nothing to be said against the argument. But when we are asked to accept the historical truth of the miraculous story of Jonah because (according to one of the Synoptists) it is alluded to by our Lord; when we are required to believe in the Davidic authorship of a particular psalm because our Lord treats it as the work of the poet-king; when we are called upon to believe in the Jewish theory of individual guardian-angels and in the Jewish view of diabolical possession because such a belief is implied in some of our Lord's sayings (even if we are not peremptorily required to rely on the historical character and infallibility of the Old Testament *en bloc* because it is quoted by our Lord as in some sense authoritative)—the enquirer may well pause and say, "If that is the conclusion to which your principle tends, I must reconsider the whole argument." A man who has no real doubt or difficulty about these Old Testament matters may be quite satisfied when you tell him, "You must believe these things as a corollary of our Lord's Divinity." But it is otherwise with the man who has known what doubt is. "For my part," such a man will probably reply, "I regard the later date of this or that psalm, the unhistorical character of this or that Old Testament narrative, the contradiction between this or that verse in the first chapter of Genesis and modern Science, the non-messianic import of this or that prophecy, as too certainly ascertained to be set aside by any mere *a priori* reasoning such as yours. If you insist that such consequences are involved in the acceptance of Christ's Divinity, I must retrace my steps and reconsider the premises of an argument which lands me in what I can only consider a *reductio ad absurdum.*"

The difficulty which I am dealing with is one which I believe is felt to be a very real one by cultivated and philosophical minds. It is not a difficulty that is likely to be much felt by the artisan-sceptic or even by the mere man of science; their difficulties are generally of a much cruder and more elementary order. The case I am contemplating is that of a man of earnest mind and good religious training, who has read and thought too much about religious matters to suppose that Christianity has been exploded by Geology, or by the growth of that modern humanity which is shocked at the massacre of the Canaanites and the cruelties practised by David, the man after God's own heart. He has mastered, in fact, the progressive view of Revelation, and acquiesced in some more or less liberal conception of biblical inspiration. But while recognising that the conceptions of evolution, of progress, of gradual development, have to be applied to the history of Revelation, as much as to geological and secular History, he has hitherto regarded Christ as the culmination of all this stream of progressive revelation; he has regarded him as the divinely-ordained fulfiller, and not merely as the natural product of all that has gone before; as a new creation, a new beginning, the introducer of a new order of things—not as a mere link in the chain of evolution. He has come to admit the possibility of a non-genuine book having crept into the Canon; he admits the possibility of minor historical mistakes in the Evangelists, he recognises traces of human limitation, of Jewish narrowness, of exegetical misconception in the writings of the Apostles. But Christ he regards as towering above them all in absolutely solitary majesty. Before His feet alone he can still throw himself in unreserved submission and adoration. The perfectness of His character, the authority of His utterances, the Revelation of the Father which shines forth in every word and every act, still seem to him neither dulled nor dimmed by all the Science and the Criticism and the Philosophy that have tarnished the lustre of so much that once shone with absolutely flawless brilliancy for his childhood's adoring gaze. But now, when our supposed enquirer has reached this stage in his mental history, at last the question is suggested to him, "Can Jesus really be made a solitary exception to the otherwise universal law of development?" All other moral and spiritual teaching is more or less conditioned by the environment in which the teacher moves. It is, in a measure, the product of the spiritual influences that have acted upon him; however imperishable its value, it is primarily adapted only to the needs of the age to which it has been addressed. Succeeding ages invariably bring with them new needs, new problems, new social conditions to which the teaching of the past is never directly applicable. Can it be that the teaching of Jesus of Nazareth forms a solitary exception to the law which dooms the greatest spiritual inheritances of humanity to be absorbed, superseded, transcended by the spiritual productions of succeeding ages?" And then, perhaps, under the influence of this *a priori* abhorrence of the breach of continuity in human history, which has done so much to alienate religious-minded philosophers from Catholic Christianity, the enquirer betakes himself to a more close and questioning study of the Master's recorded words. The student who approaches the Gospel records in this spirit is sure to find much that will at first sight tend to confirm his doubts. He finds that the language, the framework, the intellectual atmosphere, if I may so say, of Christ's teaching is more completely Jewish than he had at first sight supposed; at every turn the imagery, for instance, of the discourses in St. John is found to be more directly inspired by the prophetic utterances than he had noticed on a superficial reading. Our Lord's whole teaching is more closely bound up than he had supposed with the Messianic idea, and when he comes to examine the genesis of the Messianic idea he finds that its origin and growth, every step in its development, and every change of form which it underwent, can be in a sense explained and accounted for as the natural outgrowth of the external circumstances or the spiritual conditions of successive ages. And then, perhaps, he acquires some knowledge of the literature of that period intervening between the close of the Old and the formation of the New Testament Canon, which has been of late so admirably dealt with in the interests of Faith by an Hulsean lecturer in this pulpit.* That literature reveals to him the fact there was more in common than he had imagined between the float-

* Professor STANTON, *The Jewish and the Christian Messiah*, 1886.

ing Messianic ideas of the time and the language which our Lord uses of Himself and His kingdom—as evidenced, for instance, by the imagery which He employed in speaking of His Second Advent. He is struck, perhaps, by some of the parallelisms between portions of our Lord's teaching and rabbinical sayings preserved in the Talmud. And then, in the light of this altered view of the relation of our Lord's teaching to the general current of Jewish thought, he comes upon distinct recognitions by the Master Himself of the Jewish beliefs about the Old Testament, about Angels, about the personal Tempter. Something like this has probably been the intellectual history of those for whom faith in the Divine Sonship of Christ has surrendered to the supposed exigencies of historical criticism. Something like this—as I find since this sermon was written—was the case with the hero of the philosophical novel which has proved the literary sensation of the present year.*

In my own mind let me say at once that none of these things are in the least inconsistent with a full acceptance of all essential Catholic teaching about the true Divinity of Jesus Christ. But there are probably many of those whose faith has broken down beneath the weight of difficulties such as we have been considering, to whom in the whole course of their religious training and theological reading this kenotic aspect of the Incarnation has not once been suggested. They have everywhere found it assumed, by believers and by unbelievers alike, that if Christ was very God of very God every utterance of his—at least if its

* *Robert Elsmere*, by Mrs. HUMPHRY WARD.

subject-matter has any connexion, however remote, with religion—must necessarily be accepted as literally, historically, and in the fullest sense infallible. It seems to me, therefore, very important that we should insist clearly and strongly that a limitation of knowledge is implied in the very idea of Incarnation. Upon reflection I suppose everyone will admit that it would have been impossible that Jesus, as he wandered in solitary communion with his heavenly Father over the hillsides of Galilee, as he stood teaching those poor simple fishermen on the border of the Lake, as he drank to the full the cup of human agony in the Garden of Gethsemane, should have all the time had his brain full of the scientific truths which ages of patient labour have revealed to a wondering world. To suppose *that* would be to make of our Lord a non-natural man, so unlike the men that we know of, as to destroy the whole purpose and meaning of the Incarnation. Such knowledge as this would have been no qualification, it would have been a positive hindrance to Him in the performance of the Father's work—in the fulfilment of the temporal mission—the οἰκονομία for which He was sent into the world. And if no reflecting Christian supposes that this anticipation of the whole march of scientific enquiry, this violent interruption of the laws of intellectual progress was necessary to our Lord's true Divinity, why should we be bound to postulate any such anticipation of the course of historical enquiry and literary research because some of their problems are accidentally connected with facts in the spiritual development of humanity? If our Lord Jesus Christ can without prejudice to His Divine Sonship be supposed to have been ignorant, and to have shown His ignorance of certain scientific facts, why should he not equally be supposed to have known only what an ordinary Jew of his day knew about the authorship of Old Testament Books, and about those facts of the unseen world which have no essential connection with the spiritual and moral life of man? At the same time, while we frankly and fully admit that Jesus Christ was not merely a man but a Jew whose intellectual conceptions were conditioned by the circumstances of his time, it is important to observe how extremely few are the cases in which we have any need to remember it. Just think for one moment how full of Jewish limitation and Jewish peculiarities is the thought of St. Paul and St. John, and then compare it with the handful of passages in which our Lord's teaching appears incidentally—without the smallest loss of its intrinsic value—to be expressed in terms of some Jewish belief which offers difficulties to the modern thinker. Our Lord's *language* is necessarily Judaic; all language is essentially human; every language bears upon its structure the impress or the mental conditions of the nation that spoke it. And between the ideas which our Lord's language implies and ours the difference is, from the spiritual point of view, little more than a difference of language. There is hardly, to my mind, a more convincing proof that Jesus Christ was more than a mere prophet than the universality of his thoughts, the absence of limitation, the universal applicability of his moral and spiritual teaching. No doubt it is well that we should shrink from prying into the mysteries of that divine-human nature; we shall never be able to picture to ourselves exactly what the consciousness of Jesus was like. But in so far as we can venture reverently to conjecture how spiritual perfection and spiritual infallibility were compatible with intellectual limitation, we may perhaps suppose that the pure spirituality of our Lord's character and thought and teaching carried with it an exemption from all limitations which could have the smallest effect on the spiritual value of what he taught. The limitations which we notice in the greatest of ordinary human teachers consist just in this—in mistaking the merely local and temporary for the universal and eternal, in mistaking the accidental for the essential, in confusing some vital spiritual truth with some external form, or some intellectual formula, in which it has clothed itself. From limitation of this kind the Christ was freed by the unique spiritual insight which the indwelling Word communicated to the human soul. His vision of spiritual truth was so unclouded that He *could* not take for spiritual something which was not really spiritual at all.

But there are other questions of what we call Theology which cannot be solved by any conceivable keenness of spiritual insight. I hope it will not be thought a paradox if I say that it was no part of our Lord's mission on earth to teach Theology. He came to teach Religion. I am not one of those who think that you can have Religion without God, or even Religion without Theology. But we must remember that Theology is a Science—a Science whose function it is to set the eternal truths of Religion in their proper relation to all other truths. The *religious* revelation, the revelation of God made by Christ, was, we believe, final and complete, though it is only (as He Himself ever taught) by the continuous revelation through the Holy Spirit that the one absolute revelation of God in Christ can be applied to the needs and problems of successive ages. But the *scientific* revelation—the revelation of Nature—it was not God's purpose to make through Christ; and a correct critical and scientific Theology was not possible when that ever-progressing and ever-expanding revelation of Nature had hardly begun. Such questions as the mode and process of Creation, the mode of God's government of the world through laws of nature and laws of mind, the chronology of his gradual self-revelation to the world—and especially to the Jewish people in the past—all these are scientific questions whose bearing upon eternal spiritual truth is but accidental. We may, indeed, see the workings of divine Providence, or, perhaps, it is better to say of the absolute spirituality of our Lord's nature, in the seldomness with which such questions are touched upon, however incidentally, in the Gospel discourses—in the complete concentration of the Master's thought upon the essential, the religious, the eternal. But for our Lord to have been supernaturally prevented from sharing and occasionally showing that He shared, scientific, historical, perhaps I may even say philosophical ideas, which have been superseded by the progress of scientific enquiry and biblical criticism—*that* would have been to destroy the reality of His human nature altogether. It would have made of Him a Gnostic emanation, and not a divine man.

I do not urge that we should vainly speculate upon the exact line of demarcation between the sphere of the natural, in which the man Christ Jesus was fallible, and the sphere of the spiritual, in which He on whom the Spirit was outpoured without measure was infallible. I do not ask that we should attempt to define scholastically the precise mode of the co-existence of the divine and human natures in the Incarnate Logos, I only ask for a reverent acceptance of facts. About what is not revealed to us let us confess our ignorance, or allow each man to speculate as he pleases; but where we do plainly find that our Lord was allowed to be ignorant of things which we know, let us neither shut our ears to the revelation of Science, nor seek to explain away the collision between that revelation and the incidental statements on non-spiritual matters of Him in whom God has revealed to us his very Self. The whole difficulty would disappear if we would frankly accept St. Luke's statement that our Lord "increased in wisdom." Increase in wisdom was only possible to one who was ignorant of some things. The medieval teachers who thought it "inconvenient" to deny the omniscience of our Lord, even *tanquam homo*, had to explain away the statement of the Evangelist, and seem practically to make the infant Jesus in the cradle at Bethlehem as fully possessed of all human knowledge as the Jesus who spake as never man yet spake.

I can imagine that some may feel a sort of doubt as to what, after all these deductions or abatements (as they may think them), is really left of the precious doctrine which I have been trying to defend by stripping it of adventitious accretions. That difficulty cannot be dealt with fully at the end of a sermon. But I should like to lay before you the words in which the position of those who maintained the limitation of Christ's human knowledge was stated by one of their most fair and thoughtful opponents in the twelfth century. To do so will perhaps be the best way of convincing you that the view which I advocate is no desperate device of a baffled nineteenth century apologist, but a view which was held in what are somewhat questionably called the ages of Faith, by divines of unquestioned Catholic Orthodoxy. This is the way their position is stated by Robert de Melun, Bishop of Hereford in the latter half of the twelfth century: "As all power is said to have been given unto Christ the man, because he had a perfect and sufficient power of redeeming and reconciling and judging the world, so also in Christ the man are said to be hidden all the treasures of the wisdom and of the knowledge of God, because he had perfect and sufficient knowledge for the administration of the aforesaid power. For it was necessary that he should have wisdom and knowledge of these things for the doing of which the manhood was assumed. But he assumed not the manhood in order that he might create or rule heaven and earth by human wisdom, but that he might conquer the devil and deliver man from his power. And since the man assumed had perfect and sufficient knowledge for the accomplishment of this, the Apostle says that in Christ the man all the treasures of God's wisdom and knowledge are hid, and not because the man assumed had as much wisdom and knowledge as the Word that assumed Him."*

Does not the exegesis of this nameless scholastic contain a useful caution for us—a wholesome doctrine and needful for these times? Do we not want to emphasise more, to bring into more prominence the practical, the spiritual, and the personal side of the great Catholic Doctrines about Christ—that Christ was a sinless Man; that his character was perfect; that that character represents to us the character of God perfectly, fully, finally; that God is speaking to us through Christ; that we may accept Christ's assurance of forgiveness as God's assurance; that God would have us be like Christ, that we can implicitly believe all that Christ tells us about God's Fatherly love of us, about His holiness, about the eternal life that is promised to those who follow Christ? It is not commonly with Christological teaching such as this that difficulties are found by the mass of reverent and intelligent enquirers. And yet, surely, it is to these comparatively simple truths rather than to the more wonder-moving and more metaphysical presentations of Christ's Divinity that the doctrine owes its power over heart and conscience, its influence over life and character. There are, of course, Agnostics who cannot believe that God is

* The treatise is printed in Bulæus: *Historia Universitatis Parisiensis*, T. II., pp. 600, 601.

revealed in Christ, because they do not believe that God is. There are those whom some highly speculative Philosophy, or the adoption of some highly destructive critical opinions, forbid to assert even this much about Christ. But these are not the majority. To the majority of Theists it is not statements such as I have just made that seem incredible or unintelligible, whatever embarrassments they may feel about their evidence. Their difficulties are firstly with the technical Trinitarian and Christological formulæ, with which they are generally associated; secondly, with the mistaken interpretations which have been given to these doctrines and the mistaken inferences which have been drawn from them. At least, it is here that the difficulties commonly begin that end by reducing Christ for so many devout and reverent minds to at best a prophet, more or less inspired, more or less deluded.

Are we then to suppress, to attenuate, and whittle down the full Catholic doctrine of the Divinity of Christ, because there are many who find difficulties in our formulæ, though they are capable of sharing the heart of our belief? I do not say so. But I do say that we should in all our teaching put the simpler presentations—the moral, the spiritual, the personal aspects of Christ's Divinity—foremost. Let us show people how Christ is a real revelation of God to *us*, and how He may be so to others. Then let us endeavour to demonstrate that the great Symbols of the undivided Church are a true and natural, though perhaps not the only possible, expression of these truths whose present meaning and significance have been already felt, that the head-truths of the Catholic Faith supply a natural basis, a reasonable formulation of the heart-truths of the Christian consciousness.

Then—at least with students or cultivated persons—we may go on to show that even the subtleties of the Athanasian Creed and the definitions of Theologians have a real and important meaning, though they are expressed in terms of an obsolete Philosophy, in a language which is not ours.

Thus perhaps those innumerable minds on which the hold of this great central truth of Christianity has been more or less weakened by difficulties such as we have been discussing, may come to recognise that the difficulties arose out of simple misunderstanding. It was not the Divinity of Christ, but the mistaken inferences that unintelligent Theologians and still more unintelligent commentators have drawn from it, that created the difficulty. One of the greatest of these hindrances and difficulties in the way of belief would be gone if the Pauline doctrine of the κένωσις, on which I have been dwelling to-day, were more often insisted upon—particularly in its application to the question of the knowledge of Christ in matters which have no real bearing upon His work as the Revealer of the Father—as the brightness of His glory and the express image of His person.

If this were more generally admitted by the Theologians who can speak with authority, I am sure that it would be a great help and a great relief to many essentially Christian minds. I am probably speaking to a few who could do something in this direction. To them I commend it as a subject of reverent study. If I shall seem to many to have spoken too crudely or even rashly, I can assure them I do not under-estimate the difficulties of the subject; but my sense of its difficulty is less strong than my conviction that if Theologians would be a little bolder in their words, their voices would reach ears which are now deaf to their appeals, and that for many souls from whom the face of God is now obscured by the mists of intellectual difficulty, the Sun of Righteousness would once again arise with healing in his wings.

IV.

THE HISTORICAL VALUE OF THE GOSPELS

Preached before the University of Oxford, at St. Mary's, 1895.

"Even as they delivered them unto us, which from the beginning were eye-witnesses and ministers of the word."—LUKE i. 2.

I PROPOSE this afternoon to make a few suggestions upon the great question of the historical value of our primary sources for the life and teaching of Christ. To the trained Theologian the idea of attacking such a subject within the limits of a sermon, or even of many sermons, might, I am well aware, present itself almost in the light of an impertinence, even on the part of a preacher who possessed any qualifications for delivering an *ex cathedra* judgment upon it. But we are not, and we cannot all be theological experts, and yet we have all got in some rough and ready way or other to face this question for ourselves if we want to attain to anything approaching intellectual clearness as to the basis of our Christian faith. For put as high as you like the place of intuition or emotion in the formation of Christian belief, there must, after all, be a certain basis of documentary or traditional evidence for intuition or emotion to work upon. Few will, at the present day, go the length of professing to discern by immediate devotional instinct the inspiration even of single books of the Old or New Testament, in any sense of inspiration which guarantees historical credibility; while for those who rely upon authority it is at least necessary to go to the pages of the New Testament to find the credentials of the authority upon which they are prepared to repose. We may perhaps look forward to the time when in their main outlines the purely critical questions involved shall be settled for us by the kind of authority to which sensible men are in the habit of deferring in other departments of knowledge, when it will as little be necessary for the average educated man to examine for himself the historical character of the Christian documents as it is necessary for him personally to investigate the evidence for the rotundity of the earth, or to be able fully and adequately to refute the Baconian authorship of Shakespeare. But such a consensus, though some approximation to it is not perhaps quite so distant as the uninformed sceptic is apt to imagine, has not arrived yet. The educated man who wishes to be able to form upon this matter the same sort of rough judgment that he endeavours to form upon any other large historical or critical questions which interest him outside his own special department of study must still examine such questions for himself, at least to the extent which is necessary to enable him to appreciate the value of the authorities which may challenge his adherence.

How then is such a person, without the training or

the leisure to become even an amateur Theologian, to arrive at any opinion upon a question so intricate and so controverted as the origin and mutual relations of the first three Gospels? If it were really necessary for the purpose which I have in view to adopt even a provisional Synoptic theory, the question would hardly be a fit subject for the pulpit, even in the hands of one who had mastered it. But fortunately for those of us who feel vitally interested in such matters without being experts in New Testament criticism, it is, I think, possible to arrive at some rough and ready answer to the question which I have proposed without committing ourselves to any detailed solution of the great Synoptic problem.

In the first place it is well just to remind ourselves of the fact that the earliest documentary evidence of the Christian story in the earliest ages lies outside the pages of the Gospel records. From the four practically undisputed Epistles of St. Paul, written some twenty years after the Crucifixion, we gather that both he and the earlier Apostles of the Circumcision were then preaching a creed which centred in the life and alleged resurrection of an historical person named Jesus of Nazareth. Few of the actual sayings of the Master are quoted, but in these Epistles we find ourselves in the presence of a very distinctive moral ideal which, in so far as it differed from the Judaism of the Christian era, purports to owe its existence to the life and teaching of this historical person. The criticism of certain wild Dutchmen [*] and one not very learned Englishman [†] which pro-

---

[*] See *e.g. Verisimilia*, by PIERSEN and NABER, 1886.
[†] The author of *The Four Gospels as Historical Records*, 1895.

nounces all allusions to Christ's life in these Epistles to be later insertions really cannot claim serious refutation. This testimony fairly weighed would, by itself, be sufficient to disprove some of the extremer theories which almost dispense with the personality of an historical Founder in accounting for the genesis of the Christian Religion—theories which are now no longer maintained by specialists, but which still seem to exercise some influence upon cultivated persons who have no particular acquaintance with the matter in hand. More testimony of the same kind may be derived from Pauline Epistles of almost equally indisputable genuineness, from the strongly authenticated first Epistle of St. Peter, and from the Apocalypse of St. John, which, though its authorship is not undisputed, is usually placed as early as 68 A.D. by precisely those critics whose theories in other directions have been most destructive. In such writings we have at least evidence enough to compel us to refer the existence of Christianity to the appearance upon the scene of history of a commanding Personality, and not to the slow evolution of a school or a movement, a mythopœic tendency or an imported Philosophy. But these books undoubtedly give us little information about the actual teaching and character of the historical Person whom they presuppose; and, as I wish on the present occasion to concentrate your attention primarily upon the question of character and teaching, I must pass on to the Gospel narrative, and for to-day to the Synoptic narrative. When we turn to the Synoptists, it will at least become evident on the face of it that we are in presence of a Personality whose life and words answer to and explain the fragments of direct teaching and biography contained in the earlier Christian literature, while they breathe a spirit in full harmony with and yet transcending the ideal —the new type of ethical tone and religious temper —exhibited by those indisputable early Christian writings. The *prima facie* aspect, if I may so say, of the Gospels is such as to convince us that we have to do with historical documents, though we must resort to criticism to determine their exact historical value.

The turning-point of New Testament criticism is the authorship of the Acts of the Apostles. If it were alleged that the Acts is a compilation of such a kind that it is impossible to argue from the authorship of one part to the authorship of another, we should indeed find ourselves confronted with one of those complicated critical problems on which we could arrive at an opinion only by elaborate personal investigation or by a consensus of experts. Fortunately this is not the case. The literary unity of the Acts of the Apostles and of the third Gospel, which clearly purports to be by the same author, is admitted by the ablest and most conspicuous at least of the critics who have argued for their second century date. Of course, in the Acts, as still more obviously in the Gospel, the writer is reproducing pre-existing materials, and unquestionably they are often reproduced with such fidelity as materially to colour the style of the composition. But it is not denied by writers like Baur and Zeller that we are entitled to treat the whole of these two books as, in a literary sense, the work of whoever wrote the journeys of St. Paul. In describing parts of these journeys (as everyone knows) the writer uses the first person. Now a careless or inartistic compiler might of course reproduce passages of a traveller's journal without seeing that the use of the first person was no longer applicable. But as these "we-passages" are pervaded by the same strongly-marked literary style which characterises the whole book, it is not possible to contend that these passages are extracts from the journal of the Physician Luke or other actual companion of St. Paul, introduced in good faith and without alteration by a later writer; nor will anyone allege that the author of the Acts was a clumsy and inartistic compiler like some of the inferior medieval chroniclers who are no doubt quite capable of using the first person in a borrowed passage without any intimation that it no longer means the author of the whole book. If, therefore, the "we" of Luke's journal is retained, it is retained, not by accident, but designedly, with a view to give the whole book the appearance of having been written by this companion of St. Paul. So much is admitted by writers of the Tübingen School. According to them, the object of this literary fraud was to represent St. Peter and St. Paul as having been from the first on terms of theological agreement and friendly co-operation, instead of being the rival authors of two bitterly opposed ecclesiastical factions. I must forbear here even to glance at the slowly accumulating evidence which has compelled the few surviving representatives of the great Tübingen School (whose services to historical criticism I have no wish to depreciate) gradually to qualify and narrow down their grand and comprehensive theory of Church history to very modest dimensions. And every modification of the Tübingen theory as a whole is so much deducted from the weight of the arguments against a first-century origin for the Acts of the Apostles. I cannot go into these arguments now. I can only invite anyone who has never considered the subject to put to himself the question whether the Acts of the Apostles strikes him as a very ingenious historical fiction, dexterously interwoven with a genuine journal of St. Luke and a few fragments of genuine tradition, or whether it is on the face of it the *bonâ fide* composition of a genuine historian—an historian who may have been, if you like, at times rhetorical, uncritical, or credulous, but an historian who had personally witnessed such scenes as he professes to have witnessed, and who, in matters lying beyond his personal knowledge, made an honest, if sometimes a free—perhaps even an imaginative—use of the best materials which he could collect. I venture to say that this is a question on which most men will be able to arrive at a fairly decided working judgment after a few hours' study, and I feel no doubt as to the answer which the vast majority of unbiassed minds will give to it. This afternoon I can only point out briefly how much we are warranted in inferring from this single datum that the Acts was the work of a travelling companion of St. Paul.

If that was the case, it cannot well have been

written much later than 85 A.D., and the third Gospel must have been written before that. In the present state of criticism it will hardly be questioned that the second Gospel represents a very decidedly earlier stage in the development of the common source or sources than the third. As to the first Gospel in its present form we are indeed warranted in inferring nothing. We must, therefore, so far as our present argument is concerned, put aside so much of the first Gospel as is peculiar to itself. We can only say that in so far as the first Gospel agrees with the second or third, the origin of their common source is thrown back in all probability to a period very much earlier than this; while in the parts common to the first and third Evangelists we may perhaps venture to add (though here, of course, we are on more disputable ground) that the first Gospel is probably, as a rule, more faithful than the third to the common original or originals. I must not, however, stray into these debatable matters. I only want just to suggest, by the way, that the difficulty of dating the first Gospel in its present form does not necessarily throw any discredit upon its fuller representation of discourses given more summarily by St. Luke, whatever may be thought of the narratives which find no parallel at all in any other Gospel.*

What, then, is the historical value of such testimony as this? In the first place it seems necessary to emphasise the fact that none of our narratives come

---

* Personally, I should not easily be persuaded that the group of parables which includes the Prodigal Son was the work of disciples or tradition.

from eye-witnesses. I put aside for the moment the fourth Gospel, though I do not do so from any personal doubt as to its substantially Johannine authorship. In the three Synoptists we are presented with three narratives, which (so far as our present arguments are concerned) are not known to proceed from eye-witnesses. I do not wish to cast any discredit upon the ancient and probable tradition that the second Gospel represents, with more or less fidelity, a compilation by St. Mark from the teaching of Peter, or upon the tradition that a work by St. Matthew is in some way or other embodied in our present first Gospel. But to some of us it will appear that discrepancies between the first Gospel and the fourth would allow us to claim an actual apostolic authorship for the present first Gospel only on condition of denying that of the fourth. In short, in the present state of criticism the Matthean authorship of the first Gospel in its present form will scarcely be asserted, and is certainly incapable of proof.

We are, then, presented with three narratives, none of which can be assumed to be by eye-witnesses, one at least of which can with confidence be ascribed to a person intimately associated with eye-witnesses, all of which (with the possible exception of portions of St. Matthew) must have been in existence in about 85 A.D., and the common basis of which must have been in existence at least twenty or thirty years earlier. What is the historical value of such data for a biography?

What would be the value of a number of modern

biographies, coincident in the main but differing in detail, which, with a similar uncertainty as to their actual authorship, could be traced back to a period of some fifty years after the death of their subject? The answer must obviously be that the value of such records would depend very largely indeed upon the character of their contents. On the one hand, we could not say, with regard to such biographies, that any single incident or saying in them is certainly and necessarily true just because it is there. Putting aside the hypothesis of wilful fraud and dishonesty, we cannot deny that a biography appearing under these circumstances might possibly contain this or that unhistorical saying or incident. If we had to do with an actual friend and associate of the hero—say, one of Napoleon's most trusted staff—we should, of course, be obliged, if we admitted his honesty, to accept his authority as final for such parts of his life as he actually witnessed, and for the general character of such expressions of opinion as he actually heard. As to details, memory might, of course, fail, but he could not have innocently invented a battle or attributed to his master great political designs at which he had never hinted. It is otherwise when the author, however careful and diligent in his enquiries, is not an eye or ear-witness, and does not tell us in detail the nature of his authorities. We cannot in such cases regard his statements as final. We may on adequate grounds reject one incident and doubt another without throwing discredit upon his general trustworthiness. On the other hand, it is clear that such an origin as we have supposed is perfectly consistent with a very high degree of historical certainty. Everything turns upon the internal consistency, the tone and manner of the narrative, its simple or rhetorical character, the presence or absence of a manifest bias or purpose or " tendency," as the phrase is.

If the narrative will stand critical examination, if the tone of the narrative is such as to discredit the hypothesis of fraud or dishonesty or extreme hagiological credulity—if the character, the life, and the conversation presented to us offer a distinct, coherent, and original picture, we shall in the main accept such a narrative with as much confidence as if it had been written by one of Napoleon's marshals himself. There might be blunders about dates, confusion of one secondary personage with another, slight exaggeration or traditional amplification even about the events of his public career, still more about his early life and family history; but we might quite probably rise from the perusal of such a narrative with a confidence, for all practical purposes absolute, that in the main we knew the sort of man that Napoleon was, the way he lived, and the way he talked.

I need hardly say that a very large part of our knowledge of some of the best-known characters of ancient history, if not of modern, rests upon evidence very much of this character. We criticise freely the biographies of the Roman emperors in Suetonius or the Augustan history, but no sensible man doubts the nobleness of Trajan or the villainy of Commodus. Reject all evidence but that of eye-witnesses or historians whose sources of information are detailed, and what should we know about any of the leading figures in ancient history, except Cicero and one or two of his contemporaries?

Now let us turn to the biographies of our Lord. In one respect the comparison which I have instituted does injustice to them. The Jew was accustomed to preserve the teaching of a Master for many generations with substantial accuracy. Our knowledge of this fact makes a far greater degree of exactness in the transmission of teaching possible and even probable *a priori* than could be looked for in modern times. Still, the facts being what they are, we cannot say that it is impossible that this or that incident may be unhistorical, this or that saying misrepresented or misunderstood, or even evolved by the unconscious working of traditional development. It is possible that critical comparison of one Synoptist with another, or a strong sense of the intrinsic improbability of such and such an act, or of its incongruity with the character revealed by better attested narratives, may compel us to doubt or to reject this or that particular incident or saying of Christ. And we may do so without necessarily throwing doubt or discredit upon the rest. That is done by every historian who criticises his authorities. Of course, if the result of such critical examination is to reveal more than a certain amount of inconsistency in the same authority, or conflict between parallel authorities, the result might be seriously to weaken our confidence in their general value. But the critical treatment of authorities by no means necessarily has this effect. I think it is of great importance to insist strongly upon this simple principle. However little we have set ourselves down to a systematic study of the Gospel narratives, we cannot help, many of us, as we listen for instance to the reading of the Bible in church, suspecting this or that detail, especially when we have observed that it represents an amplification, and a less probable amplification, of another Synoptist. Now, when once we have outlived our childhood's confidence that a thing must be true simply because it is in the Bible, such suspicions or rejections are apt to throw a film of doubt over our whole mental pictures of the Christ in whom we have believed. Let us, then, realize distinctly that critical rejection of details does not necessarily throw doubt upon the rest. In no sphere is the "all or nothing" argument more hopelessly irrational. Indeed, it is a mode of treatment which no one adopts in any ordinary historical enquiry. Yet it has, for instance, been said that we cannot be sure that any one recorded saying of Christ is actually His. Such scepticism seems to be excessive, but we might admit it without seriously weakening our belief in the historical character of the Gospel narrative. We might not be sure that any given saying is genuine, but we might still be quite sure that by far the larger part of them are so.

Let us recur once more to a modern parallel. When a great man disappears from among us, the air is full of anecdotes about him or sayings attributed to him. Some of them, in all probability,

THE GOSPELS

are not true. But so far is the rejection of one from throwing doubt upon the rest, that it is positively impossible to account for the production of this or that apocryphal story except upon the hypothesis that many of them are true. They owe their existence to the impression created by the rest. This or that story may be rejected for want of sufficient evidence, or because really inconsistent with a fuller knowledge of the man's character. In many cases, no doubt, we may, we must, remain ignorant as to exactly which stories are true and which are apocryphal—as to the exact degree of exaggeration or pointing which some of them may have undergone. But a great deal of doubt as to the details is quite consistent with a perfectly truthful general impression as to the character, opinions, and habits of the man. The sayings and doings revealed in an anonymous biography written fifty years after the man's death may reveal to us a character, a mind, a personality, a career, whose originality, whose internal consistency—I may add whose *a priori* improbability—is such as to make the hypothesis of fiction or mythical evolution, conscious or unconscious, impossible to any sane or sober critic. If Boswell had appeared anonymously fifty years after Dr. Johnson's death, with all the personal authentication of its contents eliminated, the fact would hardly have affected our judgment as to the book's substantial historical value, though it would doubtless allow us greater scope for a critical treatment of details. I want reverently to suggest that we are in very much this position with regard to the main outlines of the life and the character of Him whom we believe to have been the Son of God. On the present occasion I must not follow out this suggestion any further. But I must add one word of explanation. I have purposely refrained from introducing the difficulties arising from what is commonly called the supernatural character of some events in the recorded life of Christ, or of some of the claims which He is recorded to have made for Himself. I do not do so because I think our belief on such matters indifferent. I strongly feel that the fact that Christ claimed to work cures is so intimately bound up with the very woof and fibre of narrative and discourse alike as to place it beyond the reach of sober criticism, however you may interpret that fact. But it is manifest that the question of ascribing to Christ more than the normal human control over nature, or of ascribing to Him in any distinctive sense a divine Sonship, cannot even be considered until we are convinced that the character and the teaching with which we are presented in the evangelic narratives are substantially historical and not fictitious, and until we are persuaded that in this character and this teaching we are face to face with a phenomenon unique in human history and unique in its present spiritual significance.

And these two convictions cannot altogether be separated. Our judgment upon the historical character of the evangelical picture must depend largely upon our power of appreciating the spiritual significance of that picture. It is, as the now despised Paley contended long ago, the originality of

THE GOSPELS

the character of Christ which constitutes the greatest of all guarantees of its historical existence. We have only to compare the Gospels even with other New Testament writings to see how wide is the spiritual and intellectual gulf which separates Christ from the greatest of his Apostles.* None of them were capable of inventing one of the more striking and characteristic of the sayings of Christ; no one of them ever so much as attempted to write a parable.†

* Cf. the declaration of J. S. Mill (*Essays on Religion*, Ed. iii. 1874, p. 253): "The most valuable part of the effect on the character which Christianity has produced by holding up in a Divine Person a standard of excellence and a model for imitation is available even to the absolute unbeliever, and can never more be lost to humanity. . . . Whatever else may be taken away from us by rational criticism, Christ is still left; a unique figure, not more unlike all his precursors than all his followers, even those who had the direct benefit of his personal teaching. It is of no use to say that Christ as exhibited in the Gospels is not historical, and that we know not how much of what is admirable has been superadded by the tradition of his followers. The tradition of followers suffices to insert any number of marvels, and may have inserted all the miracles which he is reputed to have wrought. But who among his disciples or among their proselytes was capable of inventing the sayings ascribed to Jesus, or of imagining the life and character revealed in the Gospels? Certainly not the fishermen of Galilee, as certainly not St. Paul, whose character and idiosyncrasies were of a totally different sort; still less the early Christian writers, in whom nothing is more evident than that the good which was in them was all derived, as they always professed that it was derived, from the higher source."

Mill limits these remarks to the discourses in the Synoptists. A deeper study of the discourses of the Fourth Gospel, which Mill treats as "poor stuff," would have revealed beneath the mannerism and the expansion which is due to the narrator a not less valuable deposit of self-evidently original matter.

† "Among early uninspired Christian writers there were several imitators of the apostolic Epistles; but only one, Hermas, who attempted to imitate the parables, and that with such poor success that we need the less wonder that others did not try the experiment."— SALMON, *Introduction to the New Testament* (1881), p. 136.

But these are arguments which can, of course, only appeal to people who are capable of appreciating this spiritual differentia, if I may so call it, of Christ's life and words. And, therefore, we must recognise that there is after all some logical justification for those who find in their own instinctive perceptions a sufficient basis for their Christian belief. They believe that Christ was what He is represented to have been simply because they cannot believe otherwise. Its existence as a fiction or unhistorical tradition would be more unintelligible than its existence as fact, and they go on to infer that being what He was He must have been the Son of God, because they cannot believe that there can be anything diviner than such a character and such a life. Such an attitude is perfectly defensible, certainly in persons who do not feel either the inclination or the capacity for more detailed intellectual investigation. They have the right to ignore objections and difficulties on matters of detail, just as full a right as we have to enjoy and to accord a general acceptance to any ordinary biography, while aware that not unreasonable doubts may have been felt about details by those who have the leisure and inclination for critical investigation. But I do also very earnestly wish to assert the right of those who cannot but feel that parts of the Gospel narrative do not stand historically upon the same basis with the rest—who cannot but feel as they compare one Synoptist with another that the first Gospel has the right version of such and such a saying and St. Luke a wrong one, that this miracle has been exaggerated

THE GOSPELS

and that is a piece of "aftermath"—to say so freely without being charged with destroying either for themselves or for others a reasonable basis for their belief in a unique revelation of God through the historic Christ. The great question in what that uniqueness consists, I shall hope to treat on some future occasion.

Meanwhile let me just suggest this one thought. I have confined myself chiefly to the record of Christ's character and to the words in which most conspicuously that character was manifested. That is the basis upon which must needs be based any further inferences as to who and what Jesus of Nazareth actually was. I do not deny, I strongly feel, the deep importance of many of the speculative questions which may arise in this connexion. But do not let us fall into the way of treating the character of Christ as a mere *evidence* of divine revelation. The character of Jesus Christ is itself surely the great revelation of God. If we cannot find in the character of Jesus, as it is presented to us in the pages of the Gospels, a revelation of the highest, we must not expect to find any historic testimony or any metaphysical reasoning which can possibly compel our belief in such a revelation. The character of Christ and the conviction that that character represents God—that is the heart of the Christian faith; that is what affects the life. Lay hold upon that character, live in its light, seek to reproduce it in your lives, and it is a matter of comparative unimportance—*comparative* unimportance except so far as it affects your power of co-operation with the great mass, the organized Ecclesia of Christian believers—whether or no you express that faith in the traditional terms of Christian Theology, or in the formulæ of later Philosophy, or in the homeliest language of the most commonplace religious experience.

V.

THE UNIQUE SON

Preached in Balliol College Chapel, 1894.

"In this was manifested the love of God towards us, because that God sent his only begotten Son into the world, that we might live through him."—1 JOHN iv. 9.

BISHOP LIGHTFOOT has pointed out that the true meaning of μονογένης is not so much "only-begotten" as "the only one of his kind."* The emphasis is entirely on the μονο, not at all on the γένης. In the Epistle of St. Clement of Rome the word is applied to the Phœnix, that fabulous bird which was supposed to be the only living specimen of its kind, and to die every 500 years, leaving an egg which, hatched (according to one version of the story) by the heat of its parent's funeral pyre, produced a new bird to carry on the solitary succession. The story—implicitly believed alike by cultivated pagan writers and by Christian Fathers—exactly illustrates the meaning which it originally bore in Christian Theology. There was never more than one Phœnix at a time: that solitary individual formed, as it were, a kind by itself. So when St. John applied the term

* On Clement of Rome, *Ad. Cor.* I. 25.

to Jesus Christ, he meant to indicate that the expression "Son of God" is used of Him in a sense in which it can be applied to none other. There was and could be but one "Son of God" in this supreme sense. Jesus Christ was the only Son of that kind. The force of the word was correctly appreciated by the earlier Latin versions of the Creed, in which it is translated by "unicus," the "only" or "unique Son": it is only in later versions that we find the less accurate "unigenitus" or "only-begotten."

The idea of the "eternal generation" of the Son is, no doubt, one of the most puzzling and difficult of theological technicalities. Perhaps part of the endless perplexities which it has created may be removed by simply going back to this its original meaning. Originally and historically the word was used to express this fundamental and all-important, but surely not unintelligible Christian idea, that Jesus Christ was the Son of God in a sense in which no other being ever was or can be. He represents God, he reveals God's nature in a way which no other has done or (we believe) can do. His relation to God the Father, His relation to Humanity, is solitary, un-paralleled, unique; and there are, I think, not many critics of the Gospel who will not admit that no less than this, as a mere matter of history, Jesus did claim for Himself. No doubt to the Jew, "Son of God" meant primarily "the Messiah," but Messiahship (as Jesus interpreted it) did imply this universal claim.

At the present day many writers are trying, and to my mind are rightly trying, to understand and to translate into terms of modern thought the language of traditional theology about the Person of our Lord Jesus Christ. But those who make such attempts are often told both by the zealots of an uncompromising orthodoxy, and by the enemies of all constructive Theology, that they are really explaining away what was meant by the original framers of the Christian Creed. Undoubtedly there may sometimes be grounds for such complaints. The true test, as it seems to me, between a view of Christ's nature which can be regarded as a legitimate development of historical Christianity, and one which can only be looked upon as a new and different creed, is this, "Does it admit the Divine Sonship of Christ in some unique, some solitary sense, or does it make Christ merely one of many Sons of God?" Of course, I do not mean that there may not be important differences between Theologians who would agree in accepting Christ as the only-begotten Son of God in the sense which I have defined. But assuredly these differences melt into insignificance when they are compared with the broad gulf which separates those who are agreed in thinking thus of Christ and those whose theories, expressed though they may be in the rhetoric of glowing admiration, yet end by reducing Him to *merely* one among many saints or prophets or founders of religions.

We ought, indeed, to admit—we ought most strongly to assert, that Jesus Christ is not the only Son of God. All men are born sons of God in one sense; in another all men are called to be sons of God, and may become so by accepting and appropriating to themselves the relation in which they really stand to the Heavenly Father, as it has been most completely revealed in the unique Son, Jesus Christ. It is not merely in the sense of being creatures of God or objects of his love that we may in a real sense claim that all men are sons of God. All men share the divine nature, since all have Conscience and Reason and Will. Thus, in a most real sense, every man reveals God to his fellow-man. We can only think of God at all by the analogy of man; we can only think of Him as Reason and Will and Goodness, however fully we recognise that these terms are applied to God, as the Schoolmen said, *sensu eminentiori*. Do not those who pour such lofty scorn upon anthropomorphism usually end in the mere fetishism of conceiving God in terms of matter or of force? If we feel that to think of God by the analogy of what is highest in the Universe is at once more rational and more reverent than to liken Him to what is lowest, or to the simply unintelligible, we must admit that in a very real sense indeed every human soul reveals God. God is in a manner reproduced in every man; so far he is a son of God. And in a still higher sense every good man in proportion to his goodness reveals God to his fellow-men. The highest that we know in man is the highest that we can think of God. Even a Philosopher who objects to speaking of God as moral admits that he possesses something much better than morality. And what can this word "better" mean to us but a higher degree of the goodness which we have learned to reverence in men? In Jesus Christ Humanity attained its highest moral development, and just because of that perfect Humanity the conscience of mankind has recognised in him a supreme, a unique, in a sense a final revelation of that God who all through the world's history had been, by slow, successive stages, revealing Himself more and more fully to the human spirit.

There are some people to whom the formulæ of technical Theology are so sacred, that it seems almost a profanation to attempt to explain or even to understand them. There are others to whom they have come to seem so arid and repellent, that if anyone finds a meaning there which is capable of reaching the understanding or the heart, they will promptly tell him that the meaning cannot really be there. This state of mind might be curiously illustrated by some of the comments that have been made upon the Theology of Robert Browning. It is hardly denied that Browning's whole being was penetrated with this idea of Christ as the supreme revealer, the one paramount representative of God to man. And yet we have been told by his biographer* that, though he uses the language of Christian Theology, his declarations cannot of course be understood in the sense of orthodox Christianity. Why of course? If we tried to get to the bottom of the old phrases in which orthodox Christianity has become stereotyped, we should find perhaps sometimes that the burning words of a nineteenth century poet are after all only the present-day equivalent of the thoughts and words of a St. John in the first

* Mrs. SUTHERLAND ORR.

century, and of an Athanasius in the fourth. If there be any truth in the way in which I have attempted to explain this tremendous phrase, "the only-begotten Son of God," the thought which they contain is one of which Robert Browning's poetry is simply full. No doubt in one sense no age can think about Christ exactly as any other age has thought. It has not been so in the past; it is unreasonable to expect that it will be so in the future. But we do not worship a different God in manhood because our thoughts about Him are different from what they were in childhood. God is not less God to us, but more God, because the thoughts about Him have grown with our growth. And so we do indeed want, as it has been boldly said, to reconceive the Christ. Only let us not assume at starting that the Christ when reconceived and represented to the thoughts of our own age or of the next, will be essentially a different Christ from the Christ of Christian Theology, or that his Divinity will mean less to us than it did to our fathers, because other language than that of technical Theology may sometimes come most naturally to our lips when we try to make articulate to ourselves what we think and feel about Jesus Christ, and because not until we have so explained it does the traditional Theology of itself become once more living thought to us.

> "That one face, far from vanish, rather grows,
> Or decomposes but to recompose."*

* BROWNING, Epilogue to *Dramatis Personæ*.

I have insisted upon this idea of the uniqueness of Christ's position for two reasons. First, on account of its theoretical importance. There are other questions about the Person and Office of Christ (to use the technical theological terms) which many of you will feel to have no intimate bearing upon the spiritual life. At all events you feel that you have not the knowledge, nor the time necessary for acquiring the knowledge, to answer them now. Some, even among religiously-minded men, will always be content to leave many of them to professed Theologians. But this question, "Was Christ merely *a* good Man and *a* great Teacher, or was he something more? Is he to be to us simply one of many teachers, to be discarded possibly sooner or later because, however valuable in the past, the world is destined more and more to outgrow His teaching? Is He to be merely one of many, or are His claims upon us unique, supreme, paramount?"—this is a question which I do not think you can afford to leave wholly unanswered. To this extent the question, "what think ye of Christ?" is one which you must face. To leave it on one side is virtually to negative any exceptional claim on Christ's part. It is necessary even for mere intellectual clearness in our view of the world's history, that we should give some sort of answer to this question. No doubt this conviction that Jesus was in some supreme sense the Son of God cannot rest on merely intellectual grounds alone. It is only by some measure of sympathy that we can understand or enter into the character of another. Except by the analogy of our own experience it is impossible even to assure ourselves of the existence of another soul, still less to enter into its feelings and thoughts and aims. There must be something in us capable of responding to the appeal which the ideal supremely realized in Christ makes to the conscience before we can say for ourselves, "Truly this was the Son of God!" But there are, I think, very many who do really respond to the moral appeal of Christ, who do practically strive to take the life and teaching of Christ as the one supreme exponent to them alike of the mind of God and of human duty, who yet find it difficult to attach a definite meaning to the language in which the Church has formulated its beliefs about Christ; they feel that there is a certain gulf between their practical working convictions and the language which, in worship, the Church puts into their mouths. To such minds it may perhaps be a help to see that, whatever else may still remain obscure or doubtful to them, those who do in their hearts accept Christ in this way as the supreme revealer of the divine ideal of human life, are fully entitled to call Him, as St. John called Him, the only-begotten Son of God.

And then let me add one word as to the practical importance of this doctrine. Doubtless there are many who profess that intellectually they cannot regard Christ as anything but a good man of commanding religious genius, who yet do practically in their own personal life never think of God except as the sort of Being whom Christ has made us feel Him to be, and whom the world before Christ never did feel Him to be. There are others who cannot accept the Christian or, perhaps, any other view of God's nature, who yet are content practically to make the imitation of Christ their moral ideal. Doubtless, Christ has been and is the light of thousands of those who do not call upon His name. But, nevertheless, these inadequate views of Christ's nature and claims upon us do tend in the long run to weaken—though they need not always destroy—the supremacy of the Christian ideals in our hearts and in our lives. The moment we put Christ simply in a line with other thinkers and other teachers, we assume an attitude of criticism towards Him. And that attitude of criticism is one which it is difficult to reconcile with the attitude of loyal and unreserved acceptance and discipleship by which the Christian faith has wrought its great spiritual triumphs. I do not mean, of course, by this that Christ claims any renunciation of individual reason or conscience. To criticise is to judge; in this sense there must be criticism of Christ's claims before we accept them or before we grow into conscious acceptance of a traditional faith. There must be judging or criticising to know what Christ has actually taught; there must be judging or criticising by the conscience in its very efforts to develop and apply His teaching to our own individual circumstances and to the needs of our own age: "he that is spiritual judgeth all things." But when we have decided to accept Christ as the supreme Revealer, it is not very easy to over-estimate the spiritual gain, the oneness of aim, the concentration (if I may so say) of moral energy, which springs from the conviction that in the life and teaching and personality of Jesus Christ—and not outside them—is to be found for ourselves and for the world in which we live the saving Gospel that it is groping after.*

I had intended to conclude with a few words on the practical importance of making up our minds, so far as we can, upon this great question of the claims of Christ. But perhaps I can best suggest what I want to bring out in another way. We have just lost one who was at the time of his death, with one exception, the greatest master of the English language still left among us. Some of the press notices of the late Professor Seeley show a strangely inadequate recognition, as it seems to me, of his true place both in English literature and in English religion. The advance of criticism may have somewhat diminished the value of *Ecce Homo* as an historical study†: I do not think it has touched its usefulness as a help to practical Christianity. To many in our generation *Ecce Homo* has taught far more than such a book as *Imitatio Christi* (with all its truth and beauty) can teach to men who do not live in a medieval monastery about the practical application of our Lord's moral teaching to the spiritual needs and the everyday duties of modern life. To some of us it has come to seem almost

---

* "Division of value is always a diminution of value; so that the highest ideal must be a single ideal."—WUNDT, *Ethics*, vol. i. (E. T., 1897) p. 99.

† The advance has chiefly consisted in enabling us to appreciate better Christ's relation to Jewish history and to his environment.

like the very Gospel itself rewritten in the language of the nineteenth century. Its declared purpose is simply to constitute an historical inquiry into the ethical teaching of Jesus Christ. With Theology, strictly speaking, it does not avowedly concern itself at all. And yet the writer who summed up the essence of Christ's teaching in the famous phrase, "the enthusiasm of humanity," found that he could not give an historical account of what Christ taught or of the reasons of His success without recognising in the fullest and most explicit manner the claim to a unique personal authority which is implied as much in the Sermon on the Mount as in the Johannine version of the Master's life. A morality which is essentially bound up with a devotion to a Person is already a religion. I hardly know of any book that appeals so directly to the conscience of a man anxious, amid all difficulties intellectual and practical, to get an answer for his own soul's sake to the old question, "What must I do to be saved?" The book is throughout intensely practical, and yet it distinctly implies a Theology, a Theology which may be all the more impressive to some minds because it is more often implied than expressed. Had its author attempted to sum up that implied Theology in a sentence, he would perhaps have expressed himself in some such words as these, which I take from a like-minded writer whose name is revered in this place: "For most of us," said Arnold Toynbee, "Christ is the expression of God, *i.e.*, the eternal fact within us and without us. In time of peril, of failing, and of falsehood, the one power that enables us to transcend weakness is the feeling of the communion of the two eternal facts in Christ."*

* *Notes and Jottings*, published at the end of *The Industrial Revolution*, p. 244.

VI.

THE HISTORIC CHRIST

Preached before the University of Oxford, at St. Mary's,
1896.

"And Philip said, If thou believest with all thine heart, thou mayest. And he answered and said, I believe that Jesus Christ is the Son of God."—ACTS viii. 37.

IT is well known that these words form no part of the original text of the Acts. Our Bodleian Codex Laudianus is the only uncial MS. which contains them. But they possess an historical interest assuredly not inferior to what they would have possessed had they proceeded from the pen of St. Luke himself. For they had crept into some copies as early as the time of Irenæus. They form, beyond doubt, an extract from some baptismal service-book dating from the middle of the second century at latest, and in all probability much earlier. Creeds were, of course, originally baptismal professions of faith. Here, then, we have presented to us the earliest creed of the Catholic Church. For at least a century after her foundation the Church required from candidates for her membership—and even from candidates for her ministry—no other formal profession of faith than this: "I believe that Jesus Christ is the Son of God."

Many of us find it difficult to look back upon those early days of Christianity without wishing that the Church had never attempted further to elaborate her authoritative standards of faith. But, when we give expression to such a wish, we are sometimes met by the protest that a principle of development is of the essence of the Christian faith; that it was part of Christ's plan that His work should be carried on by His Church, and that it is unhistorical and unphilosophical to insist that Christianity shall mean no more to us than it meant to the simplest and least instructed convert in the first ages of the Church. And in recent times we find the plea for a more elaborate, a more formulated, a more dogmatic Christianity echoed in a quite opposite quarter. We hear eloquent voices calling upon us to abandon the futile attempt to get back to the historic Christ, to reconstruct His actual teaching, and to limit our conception of Christianity to belief in what He actually taught and what He historically was and did. An ideal, we are told, grows, and is not made. It may originate in a sense in one mind, but that mind is itself the product and outcome of earlier streams of thought and feeling. And development starts again the moment the new thought begins to take root in other minds; so that a generation later it becomes utterly impossible to disentangle the actual teaching of the Master from the teaching of his school—to see his ideas as he himself conceived them in entire abstraction from all that has been read into them or evolved out of them under the influence of other ideas and other environments. And it is not necessary or even desirable that we should do so. The value of the Christian ideas about God and about human life (we are assured) are not affected by the question how far they have Christ's authority. The beauty and the truth of the Christian ideal is not dependent upon the possibility of tracing back all its features to the historical Christ. Let us frankly acknowledge (it is urged) that, while undoubtedly the germ of the long development must, as an historical fact, be sought in the powerful impulse given to the religious and the moral consciousness by a man of exceptional religious genius, yet the ideal itself is of slow and gradual formation; that, though elements of it are permanent, other elements are ever changing; each Christian age has contributed something to the ever-growing treasure of the Christian Society; each has inherited all the true wealth of all the ages, while it discards the errors and the exaggerations and the limitations of its predecessors. It is our wisdom not to aim at reproducing a past which has for ever vanished, or an ideal which is essentially bound up with an intellectual and a social environment very different from ours, but to make the most of our rich heritage of Christian thought and devotion and experience, and yet to be ever ready to catch what the Spirit has to say to the Churches of our own day.

Now whether this plea for the recognition of development be urged from the ultra-dogmatic or from the idealising point of view, there can be no doubt that it does represent a very important truth. This principle of development *is* inherent in the very plan of Christianity. Had Christ really attempted in detail to anticipate and to provide for the intellectual and the moral needs of distant ages, the very attempt would have been sufficient refutation of the claims which His religion makes to permanence, to universality, to finality. It was in part just this capacity for development which constituted its uniqueness. Had "the deposit of the faith" been a hard, unyielding formula or collection of formulæ, it would have been like the unquickened seed which abideth alone. It was because it had in it the germ of a growth richer and more glorious than itself that it has become the tree in the branches whereof the nations of the earth have taken up their lodgment. This was the idea of Christianity from the very first —our Lord's own idea, unless we are to suppose the disciple so much wiser than His Master. "It is expedient for you that I go away; for if I go not away the Comforter will not come unto you." "He shall take of mine, and shall show it unto you."

It is, therefore, quite reasonable when we are told not to object to some formula about Christ's nature and work because we cannot find it in the actual words of Christ Himself or in the text of the apostolic writers. But, if we recognise that it is natural and reasonable that the Church of the fourth century should see some things about Christ and his relation to God which might not have been discovered even by St. Paul and St. John, it is completely unreasonable to limit this inspiration of development to the first century or to the fourth. The Church of Christ is not dead because General Councils have ceased to sit. Even in the fourth century Councils did but give expression and acceptance to thoughts which had originated in the solitary studies of individual Theologians, and in the consciousness of the Christian society at large. The Spirit is no less taking of Christ's and showing it to us, because the machinery of ecclesiastical Synods no longer commands the paramount or exclusive authority which the Church was once disposed to accord to it. Nor need we be alarmed if critical analysis should pronounce—

> "The life-stream rich whereat we drink,
> Commingled, as we needs must think,
> With waters alien to the source."

If we admit that God's Spirit has not worked exclusively within the limits of the Christian Church, there is no reason why we should necessarily reject either a doctrinal formula or a moral idea because it represents a fusion of some Jewish or Christian thought with the Philosophy of Plato or of Aristotle.

All this may be freely admitted—nay, emphasised. There can be no Christianity without the Church. It is the fatal mistake of Protestantism, or rather, perhaps, of some very modern forms of Protestantism, to attempt to get rid of the idea and the authority of the Church, instead of widening and elevating our conception of both. But all the same, the advocates of a dogmatic and the advocates of an undogmatic development do seem both in different ways disposed to under-estimate the importance of arriving at a true historical picture of what Jesus Christ actually was, said, did.

It is true enough, no doubt, that the traditional doctrines about the Person of Christ may none the less be true—may none the less represent the inferences which ought logically to be drawn from the facts presented by the Gospel history—because, as a matter of fact, they were not explicitly drawn till a later date. But the advocates of doctrinal development seem sometimes to forget that the value of the development must after all, in part at least, depend upon the conception of the historical facts which were formed by the people who drew these inferences. Now it can hardly be seriously denied that in certain respects the picture which the fourth century formed to itself of the nature of Christ's Personality was an unhistorical picture. More and more, as the historic environment of Christ's earthly life receded into the background, the key was lost to much in Christ's teaching which, with our richer historical knowledge and our developed instinct of historical reconstruction, we may now hope to understand. The historic Christ more and more disappeared from men's view, and was superseded by a metaphysical Christ, whose humanity was, indeed, acknowledged in word, but who lacked all the attributes of the humanity which we know. If He was still a man, He was a completely non-natural man. I do not doubt that even this one-sided development had some spiritual advantages. But, if something was gained, assuredly much was lost. We may still see in the phrases of the Nicene Creed, "Of one substance with the Father," and the like, the expression in the language of fourth-century Philosophy of a truth of which the more characteristically modern expression must be sought in the Theologians (not excluding the Poet-theologians) of our own day. But let us frankly acknowledge that such formulæ can never mean to us exactly what they meant to the men of the fourth or the fifth century.

We may believe what they tell us about the indwelling of the divine Word; we can no longer accept their practical denial of Christ's human limitations. And that means that we have got to reinterpret to ourselves the symbols of the past, as the symbols of the past themselves were reinterpretations of the simpler Creed of primitive Christianity. And to see what the Nicene Creed is to mean to us, we must go back to the actual consciousness of Christ. For our belief in the divine Sonship of Jesus must, at least, be based upon what we believe it to have meant for Him. Every age has got to reinterpret the creed which it has received in the light of its own ruling ideas; and, beyond all possibility of doubt, the ruling idea of our own age is to be found in the historical way of looking at things. Neither Theology nor Philosophy, neither dogma nor sentiment, must be allowed to prevent the individual in proportion to his opportunities, and the Church at large in proportion to her opportunities, from doing all that in them lies—honestly, laboriously, reverently —to find out what Christ was and said, and thought, and did. Upon this foundation Philosophy and

Theology may be rightly called upon to build their superstructures of gold, silver, precious stones, wood, hay, stubble; Christian dogma is the result—the necessary and indispensable result—of reflection upon the life and teaching of Christ and on the consciousness which they reveal. But other foundation can no man with any spiritual advantage lay than that which is laid by the facts of history.

And the answer which we tender to the attempts to substitute a Christ of dogmatic development for the Christ of the Gospels, we must tender also to the attempts to substitute a Christ of philosophical theory for a Christ of flesh and blood. We are sometimes invited to avert our gaze from the Christ of history to a living Christ. But for us, assuredly, an unhistorical Christ can no longer be a living Christ. It is true that elements in the Christian ideal may be no less true and no less valuable because they may not all of them have been fully developed, elaborated, and applied in the life and teaching of the historic Jesus. But it is forgotten that, as a simple matter of experience, the influence of this Christian ideal has been based upon the conviction that it was actually embodied in an historic life. True, the Christians of some ages may have dwelt comparatively little upon the actual facts of the Gospel history. Many good Christians have known little of Christ after the flesh; but, in the first place, it is not proved that those ages did not suffer grievous spiritual loss by their neglect or their ignorance, or that the Madonna of medieval imagination was a satisfactory substitute for that Christ of history which the Reformation at least began to restore to us. And, secondly, however shadowy may have been the picture which some individuals or some ages may have formed of the Man of Sorrows, it was always believed that He had really lived as their imaginations painted Him.

No generation has ever continued to adore or to imitate a Christ whom it has really believed to be unhistorical. It is true, in the words of a recent article, that "the Christs of faith are many and various, changing their features with the changing features of man."* Yes, but each of them represented an honest attempt—however uninformed—to picture Christ as He really was. And it cannot permanently be otherwise for ourselves. On its theological side, the value of Christ's life consists in the belief that here once, in the course of history, God spake to man face to face, as a man speaketh to his friend—that in the character of Jesus, as it is disclosed to us by word and act, we see mirrored the character of God, and that in His consciousness of intimate union with God, can find an assurance of God's nature and God's love such as we fail to find with equal fulness in the unassisted religious consciousness of other men. It is not (as some would suggest) that we are seeking after a sign—hankering after some external guarantee, as it were, of God's existence and His nature: certainly the revelation would be nothing to us if it did not appeal to something in us that is akin to itself. But we feel that we see in the consciousness of Christ what we cannot find in any other

* Mr. DAVID O'CONNOR in the *Contemporary Review* (September, 1896).

mind, except in those that have learned it from Him. We find Him claiming a direct communion with God, and a direct authority, such as we do not find other sober religious souls claiming for themselves. Half the value—to say no more—of the Gospel picture of Christ's religious consciousness would be gone for us if we were compelled to read in it, not what an actual human soul once felt and thought, but merely what the imagination of His disciples postulated that He must have felt. And so on the moral side the inspiring, compelling, regulating force of the Christian ideal would be gone if we were compelled to see in the Gospel picture of Christ's life and words a mere religious romance which owes much of its attractiveness (as it is sometimes hinted) to some judicious instinct of selection and of omission on the part of His followers. It is but a commonplace to say—and yet in the face of such speculation it must be said again—that of all the forces which make for righteousness the influence of personality is still the strongest. A character in a novel or a play may move us, may interest, may even in a sense inspire us, but it cannot be to us what the influence of the living person can be. Attempt to make the imitation of the Tragedian's Antigone or the Stoic's "wise man" the guiding star of your life, and you will soon feel the difference between the historic person, known and felt to be historic, and the imaginary person known and recognised as unhistorical. Better, more stimulating, more helpful a thousandfold, some struggling faulty life of warm flesh and blood that has really grappled with temptation and come out not wholly vanquished, with all its sins and all its shortcomings painted with the blackest brush that the most remorseless of biographers has ever wielded, than some imaginary portrait drawn by the selective imagination of discipleship or some frigid make-believe of modern metaphysical rhetoric! The memory of a very ordinary father or teacher would be more to us by far in the hour of temptation, in the real battle of life, would it not, than the sublimest picture that hagiological imagination ever painted, when once its fictitiousness is discovered? Better the Christ of Renan, with all his self-delusion, his exaltation, his fanaticism, his sensuous imaginings, than a Christ whom we have once suspected to be a mythical growth or a philosophic idea. We may be told to "go home and venerate the myth"—yes, for others; but for ourselves no longer when once we have found it to be a myth. More intelligible the Philosophers who cry out for another Christ than those who call upon us blindly to fall down and worship a Christ whom our Philosophy has created or our own criticism destroyed! Faith has been defined, and nobly defined, as a "voluntary certainty about things unseen"; it is not, it cannot be, a voluntary ignorance of things which we might see and know if we would but open our eyes. And therefore, while we are grateful to the Philosophers who are helping us to understand those two articles of the later Creed, "I believe in the Holy Ghost, I believe in the Holy Catholic Church," we ought to be, perhaps, more grateful to the Theologians who are helping us to reconstruct for ourselves that earliest Christian Creed, "I believe that Jesus Christ is the

Son of God "—who are helping us to see what Sonship meant to the first Christians, and above all to Christ Himself. For this must be the basis, at least, of what it means to us.

I cannot, of course, attempt to reproduce all that may be learnt from such a book as Wendt's *Teaching of Jesus*. There is probably no recent work which has done so much to help us to understand the historic Christ.[*] Let me be content with suggesting three points which will, I think, become plain to most people who read such a book with an open mind.

(1) We can assign no real meaning to the idea of the divine Sonship of Jesus unless we recognise that it contains a truth about human nature in general and its relation to God. In a sense every man is a son of God—every man has in him something of the Divine. In the reason and the will and the conscience of every man there is contained a real revelation of God, and a progressive revelation—growing as man's reason and will and conscience grow, and in a still higher sense growing in proportion as man responds in act to the demands which this rational and moral nature make upon him. And conversely this doctrine about man implies a certain view of the nature of God. Only if we believe that God has something in Him in common with the nature of man—only if we believe that He is essen-

---

[*] BEYSCHLAG'S *New Testament Theology* (E. T. by Buchanan, 1895) deserves to be mentioned side by side with Wendt. The general coincidence in results (amid minor differences) between the two writers is very remarkable. Beyschlag's treatment of Christ's actual teaching, being briefer and more attractively written than Wendt's, might be read by some who would find Wendt somewhat technical.

tially the Trinity of Power and Intellect and Goodness or Love—can we understand how he can be in any real sense revealed in man. Only if we believe that He is in some measure revealed in every man can we attach any intelligible meaning to the assertion that to one man His Spirit was given not by measure.

But (2) criticism is ever making it more and more plain that it is historically impossible, as it is spiritually disastrous, to attempt to get rid of Christ's claim to a unique Sonship. There is (I think) no fact about Christ's life about which there is so general a tendency to agreement as this—that He did claim to be the Messiah. When St. Peter made his great confession at Cæsarea Philippi, when the primitive Christian professed the same faith at Baptism, this was primarily what he meant —that Jesus was the Messiah. And in a Jew the most elementary profession of faith in the Messiahship of a crucified malefactor implied a kind of Messiahship which far transcended the ordinary Jewish conception of a merely national, if supernatural, King. And still more clearly in the consciousness of Jesus Himself it must be asserted that this claim to Messianic Sonship amounted to no less than this—a claim to a unique relationship both towards God and towards the whole human race. The conception may have grown and developed, as the development of our Lord's own consciousness threw light on His study of the prophets. Already at the Temptation the sense of Messiahship was there: already the Jewish conception of Messiahship had been transcended and spiritualised; and ever more and more distinctly the idea of the Messianic Kingdom passed into the conception of a great spiritual empire of universal significance, and eventually into an ever clearer and deeper conviction that it was somehow through His own sufferings and death, through His continued influence in the world and the relation of His followers to Him in His heavenly life, that this Kingdom of God was to be set up on earth. Of course criticism cannot prevent us from regarding all this Messianic consciousness of Christ as mere delusion if we are so minded; but it can and does (as it seems to me) leave us no alternative between recognising in this consciousness a unique spiritual fact of cosmic significance and ceasing to assign to Christ the central place that he has heretofore occupied in the world's adoration.

Christ then must be recognised as the Unique Son—the μονογένης υἱός in the true and original sense of that term*—not only on account of His actual place in history, but also on account of His exceptional consciousness of a filial relation to God and of God's fatherly relation to Him. His knowledge of God's nature, His sense of God's Fatherhood, His sense of a divine mission, His perception of the true ideal for man, His realization of that ideal in actual life—all were such as none had ever known before.

(3) But thirdly, when this has once been admitted, when once we have admitted the solitary majesty of the religious and moral consciousness of Jesus, we ought

---

* See above, p. 77.

to go on to insist that all He claims for Himself He claims also for the whole human race through Him. It was the very object of His life to communicate to others also this consciousness of God's love, this consciousness of Sonship, this power of doing God's will that He experienced in such supreme wise in the depths of His own soul. We should feel less difficulty perhaps than is sometimes found in those Johannine discourses of Christ about His relation to the Father, if we noticed sufficiently that everything, or (to be quite safe) nearly everything—that the Johannine Christ claims for Himself He claims for His followers too in the measure of their actual consciousness of it —with just this difference, that it was through Himself and His teaching that He felt it possible for other men to attain in whatever measure they should attain to that walk with God of which He was conscious. Everywhere, with this solitary and yet momentous difference, there is an exact parallelism between what Jesus says of Himself and what He reveals about the true relation of others to God, however little they may know or realize it. "The Father loveth the Son ... the Father himself loveth you." "As the Father hath life in himself, even so gave he to the Son also to have life in himself." "Verily, verily, I say unto you, he that believeth hath eternal life. Because I live, ye shall live also." "He that believeth on me, the works that I do shall he do also, and greater works than these shall he do." "I and my Father are one." "Whosoever shall confess that Jesus is the Son of God, God abideth in him and he in God." "I have overcome the world." "Whatsoever is born of God overcometh the world." "To as many as received him gave he power to become the sons of God." To make men feel the love of God as He felt it, and do the will of God as He did it—that is the supreme object of Christ's revelation to the world.

And does not experience confirm this claim of Christ—the experience of history at large, the experience of saints, whatever poor experience the humblest beginner in the Christian life among us may possess about such things. It were unprofitable to speculate how near the saints of God have attained to what Christ attained. But this much is certain—that the nearer they have reached, the more fully they would have acknowledged that they attained it through Christ and what He taught. Many of us, no doubt, first realize to some extent what the Christian ideal is—I mean not merely as an external rule of life, but what the Christian character is in its relations both to God and to man—by seeing it embodied in some living, or at least in some modern, follower of Christ. Many of us find in some half-dozen modern biographies the most bracing spiritual reading that we know. But it is after all by revealing Christ that such men themselves become revealers of God to other men. The best that they have in them came from Christ. They have felt the consciousness of sonship because Christ felt it first. The best that they do for others is to lead men to Christ.

Christ then was *the* Son of God by what in actual fact He felt Himself to be, not merely by what the world has come to believe about Him. But, when once the unique character of our Lord's consciousness is admitted as the germ of the Christian development, we may quite reasonably regard the historical circumstances of His appearance and the historical consequences that have followed that appearance as confirming and establishing the position which Christian Theology assigns to Christ. Some people seem to hesitate to recognise Christ's claim to a solitary Sonship, and to lose the clearness and concentration of religious feeling which results from that recognition, not because they think that any other man that had ever lived, or is likely to live, can actually dispute His religious and moral supremacy, not because they really wish to put anyone else in His place as Lord and Master, but because they cannot get rid of the feeling that it is to some extent an historical accident—that it is due to the combination of the favouring circumstances that preceded and followed His appearance that the great spiritual revolution implied in Christianity connected itself with the name of this particular Jewish teacher. They seem afraid lest the recognition of Christ's supreme position should be inconsistent with the idea of religious evolution before Christ and after Christ. Does not such an attitude spring at bottom from an unwillingness to recognise in history the will of a personal God? If as a matter of history it is through Christ alone that we have come to the highest knowledge that we have of God, and the highest conception of that ideal which He wills for man, that can be no mere accident. To anyone who believes in God, such a relation of one historical character to God and man can be no mere chance product of evolutionary forces.

Granted, if you like, that we cannot disprove the possibility of an unknown, undiscovered Christ in some remote backwater of history, granted that the Father might (had it pleased Him) have revealed Himself through some other life (the Schoolmen were wont to debate such questions), surely it is enough for us that He has not done so. An unknown revelation, it is clear, would be no revelation at all. Admit, if you like, the speculative possibility of another Christ yet to come: surely it will be time enough to consider such unmotived possibilities when anyone can actually—I will not say realize in detail—but present us with some intelligible suggestion of any higher conception of God than is implied in Christ's revelation of God's Fatherhood, or any higher conception of human life than is implied in His ideal of Sonship to God and Brotherhood to all men. Christ was the first to present us with that ideal in its fulness. All subsequent realizations of it have sprung out of His: surely that is enough for us. Granted that Christ was made possible by a long course of religious evolution, and that a long course of religious evolution has been necessary to give Him the significance which He actually possesses for the world of to-day, and to develop in detail the ideal which originated with Him, that is no objection to our recognising in the historic Christ a supreme act of God's self-communication to the world; it is no objection except when evolution is thought of, not as the work of God, but as a substitute for God. It is very largely indeed just because it does thus emphasise the personality of God, that the idea of his definite self-revelation to and by one Man at a definite time in human history is so valuable to us. A God who is only a tendency, or a law, or a force, or an unconscious I know not what, which after long and complicated unconscious strivings at last attains to consciousness of Himself in man—such a God, we may admit, can only be supposed to reveal Himself in a process or a tendency, for He is only a name for the process or the tendency itself. Only, if He is personal—a Mind, a Thinker, a Will—can He be supposed to reveal Himself in one Person more than another. A God who is a Person may reveal Himself in one man—not in one man exclusively, but to and in one man in a pre-eminent and paramount manner at a particular moment of human history, selected and predestined just because it was the moment fitted for the development of the ideas which in germ and essence were present in the consciousness of the personal Revealer.

But, it may be asked, have you not proved too much? If the value of our belief in Christ lies largely in this, that it safeguards the belief in a personal God and Father, is it not enough to believe in such a God, whatever we think about the historical facts of Christ's life and consciousness? Is it not enough to believe that the Christian ideal of character is the revelation at once of God's nature and of man's duty, no matter how that Christian ideal historically grew up? Well, it is quite true that we should not aim at widening the gulf between ourselves and those who believe all that we believe about God, even if they are unable to see in the historic Christ any supreme incarnation of the God whom they thus conceive. If it is impossible to make an idol of Christ, there is a real danger lest we should make an idol of what is called Christology. Never let us forget that the value of our belief about Christ lies in what it helps us to believe about God, and to realize imperfectly in our own lives. Loyalty to Christ, in Christ's own teaching, always means acceptance of his teaching and fulfilment of his commands. But it is matter of experience that this belief about Christ as the historical Son of God does really help us both in thought and in worship and in life. Certainly acceptance of Christ's ideal of life is the great thing; but it helps us to believe that this ideal was once proclaimed by one who felt that He had authority to teach it, and who realized in His life all that He taught.

It is so much easier to believe in and to be loyal to a person than to an idea. I may perhaps best express what I mean by means of an analogy. It is no doubt impossible to believe in duty as the will of God unless we first believe in duty. We must believe in an eternal, ineffaceable, essential difference between good and evil before we can look upon the good as commanded by a God who is essentially good. And yet does not conscience become a totally different thing to those who hear in its dictates the voice of God? Belief in God presupposes belief in morality, and yet belief in morality almost necessitates—certainly it desiderates for its own perfection—a belief in God. Even so it is impossible to believe in the revelation of God through Christ without believing that God is a Person; and yet nothing can so strengthen and cultivate that belief in God as a Person capable of loving and of being loved—nothing can so tend to strengthen the hold of that supreme truth upon the heart and the will—as the conviction that He who reveals Himself in some measure in the conscience of every man is present pre-eminently, uniquely, eternally, in the consciousness of the Man whom He appointed. To believe in the Son makes it so much easier to believe in the Father.

VII.

REVELATION BY CHARACTER

Preached before the University of Oxford, at St. Mary's,
1894.

"Our sufficiency is of God; who also made us sufficient as ministers of a new covenant; not of the letter, but of the spirit: for the letter killeth, but the spirit giveth life."—2 COR. iii. 5, 6.

THE Christian Revelation has two aspects—a moral aspect and a theological aspect. There is a revelation about God and his nature, and there is a revelation about man and his duty. But these two revelations cannot, of course, be looked upon as standing side by side, in entire independence of one another. We cannot look upon the Christian Revelation as containing on the one hand a body of theological propositions, and on the other hand a body of moral precepts, which last have no connexion with the former, except as being the commands of the Being to whom the theological propositions relate. That is a mistake which has often been made in the history of Theology, but it is one which, in its cruder forms, is little likely to be made at the present day. It is, indeed, the essential characteristic of the Christian Revelation that it brings God and Man together, or, rather, that it declares and sets forth the eternal fact that God and Man in the divine scheme of things were always thus united. Whatever be the nature of God, that must necessarily be the ideal of human life and character. What God is, that man was eternally meant to be. In revealing the Divine Nature, Christ was necessarily revealing human duty: in setting forth the true ideal of human life, Christ was necessarily revealing the eternal nature of God. Man has never been able to form a higher ideal of God than was supplied by his highest ideal of humanity, though, alas! his ideal of God has too often fallen below his ideal of man. The pagan religions, at certain moments and in certain aspects, as we are constantly told even to exaggeration, had little connexion with morality: and a great Philosopher has recently drawn a picture of the Absolute which seems to some of us to fall as much below the lowest of current moralities as the morality of Plato soared above that of the deities which were worshipped in his time.* But for those who believe that truth is one and not many, for those to whom all human knowledge is not a mere "appearance," God can as little be above morality as he can be below it. For them a revelation of God (if such a revelation there be) must needs be a revelation of duty; a revelation of goodness must needs be a revelation of God.

That God is revealed after a unique manner in Christ is and must always be the central truth of any Christianity that can aspire to be regarded as in any

* Cf. above, p. 14.

sense an absolute, a permanent, or a final religion. But as to the method and character of that revelation, as to what revelation means, it is impossible for any but a very superficial observer to doubt that a great change is coming over the religious thought of our time, as much with many of those who repudiate as with those who welcome the idea of theological progress or development. It may help us, I think, to clearer views on this momentous subject if we confine ourselves for a moment to the purely ethical side of this revelation. To many minds the very idea of a revelation in ethics raises a host of difficulties. I will not dwell upon the efforts which have been made to show that the teaching of Christ contained nothing new. For in truth the attempt to pick Christianity to bits, and to show that each bit of it taken by itself was anticipated by such and such an ancient seer or thinker, is as great an anachronism as that atomistic view of human nature which can see in the human mind nothing but an aggregate of isolated ideas or feelings or impressions or whatever they may be called, jostling up against one another *in vacuo* as it were, and in human society nothing but a collection of isolated individuals, each of which is what he is entirely apart from his relation to the rest. In the fashionable cant of the day we might say that the teaching of Christ must be looked upon as an organic unity, not as a mere aggregate of disconnected precepts. And, though no intelligent Theologian will conceive that he has any interest in denying the approximations to Christian teaching which may be found in previous thought, whether

Jewish, Greek, or Oriental—though no one who believes that morality is rational will wish to minimise the common element which is to be found in all the higher ethical and religious teaching of the world—no serious thinker, I suppose, of the present day will care to deny that, taken as a whole, Christianity was a new thing in the world—a new thing not to be accounted for by any mere conglomerate of previous systems, or by any theory of spontaneous evolution which leaves out of account the personality or the originality of its Founder.

It is of more importance to consider some of those difficulties which are based upon the very nature of morality itself. To any system of moral rules claiming to be of universal validity, whether they are supposed to be independent deliverances of the moral consciousness or whether they are referred back to some wider principle of social utility, a whole host of objections necessarily springs up. Moral rules, it may be said, must necessarily be relative to time and place. A rule of action most expedient in one age must become wholly inexpedient in another. The most far-seeing moralist cannot anticipate the march of events and lay down the rules of action which will be demanded by a social system yet unborn. Were he to succeed in such an anticipation, it would be at the cost of becoming simply unintelligible, or worse than unintelligible, to the men of his own and of the immediately succeeding generations. And then, if we confine ourselves to one age, one country, one set of social conditions, what, it may be asked, is the real utility of a body of rules? There are no rules which admit of no exceptions. The attempt has often been made to find moral rules of less width than the general principle of promoting the general good and the most equal distribution of it—which shall admit of no exceptions, and the attempt has in general conspicuously failed; that is to say, the attempt nearly always fails, except when we import into the terms of our moral prohibition the absence of those conditions which might justify the act otherwise forbidden. The rule against lying undoubtedly admits of no exceptions, supposing we agree to exclude from the category of lying all untrue statements which are not condemned by the enlightened conscience, the untruths of politeness or of sarcasm, the untruths that we tell to the madman or the would-be assassin, the untruths of the actor and of the duly authorised detective. "Thou shalt do no murder" has no exceptions if we say that killing is no murder when it is done in self-defence, in lawful war, or at the behest of the civil magistrate. And, if the seventh commandment be quoted as an instance of a prohibition to which the highest morality knows of no exception, there is still the difficulty of defining the conditions of lawful marriage; for there are many points of matrimonial law upon which Christian Churches of the most undeniable orthodoxy have wavered considerably, and are not entirely agreed even now. How then are we to get over this difficulty inherent in any attempt to formulate the moral law even for the men of a single age or a single country? Are we compelled to give up the effort, even the tentative effort to formulate approximations to moral rules, and to abandon morality entirely to the momentary, uncalculating, unreasoning caprice of each individual moment and each individual agent? We may, I think, help ourselves out of the difficulty by appealing to a writer who, though utilitarian and completely naturalistic, has in this matter seen deeper into the heart of the spiritual life than is common with his school. He admits that the solution of our difficulty was first effected by Christianity. "The clear enunciation of one principle," says Mr. Leslie Stephen, "seems to be characteristic of all the great moral revolutions." And the new principle which Christianity introduced, he goes on to say, "may be briefly expressed in the phrase that morality is internal. The moral law, we may say, has to be expressed in the form, 'be this,' not in the form, 'do this.' The possibility of expressing any rule in this form may be regarded as deciding whether it can or cannot have a distinctively moral character. Christianity gave prominence to the doctrine that the true moral law says 'hate not,' instead of 'kill not.' The men of old time had forbidden adultery; the new moral legislator forbade lust."* So again in the case of veracity, the external rule, "lie not," *has* exceptions unless we define lying as speaking an untruth except under such and such circumstances—circumstances which can never be so precisely defined as to anticipate every possible case of moral perplexity. On the other hand, the internal rule, "be truthful" or

* *The Science of Ethics* (1882), p. 155.

"love the truth," has no exceptions. The only universal rules are rules of character. The truth-loving man—the man who would feel a pain in telling a lie, even in obedience to the rarest and most imperative demands of social duty—he and he alone can be trusted never to relax the rule of veracity except either in obedience to conventions which really alter the meaning of current language, or at the behest of some supreme duty of humanity or justice. When such a man tells an untruth, he loves not truth the less, but humanity the more. The only eternally valid rules are rules of character; and beyond a certain point character cannot be prescribed or defined by rules at all. Character must, no doubt, be revealed by word or act, but the word and act alike do but suggest the character; they do not exhaustively unfold or define it. Neither the widest formula nor the most elaborate system of moral precepts could ever by itself make a character live before the mind's eye. A character can be understood only as a whole; and it has to be understood rather by the instinct of sympathy than by the logical understanding alone.

There is another reason why morality cannot be reduced to a system of rules. The difficulty which I have already noticed is fatal to any attempt to claim for moral "intuitions," as they are called, an unexceptionable validity so long as intuitions are regarded as rules prescribing the details of conduct independently of circumstance or consequence. It cannot be rational to act without considering the consequences: indeed, no one has ever succeeded in distinguishing between an act and its consequences. The consequences, in so far as they can be foreseen, are part of the act; and our moral judgment of an act must necessarily be dependent upon the whole series of events which are intended by the agent. The real objection to Utilitarianism lies, as used to be said by our great ethical teacher,* not in its regard for consequences, so much as in the nature of the consequences to which it has usually limited its view. Pleasure is *a* good, but it is not *the* good. And yet when we ask what the good is, what is that blessed life for all mankind at which every human action ought to aim, we can as little give a perfectly adequate or final answer as we could *a priori* lay down final and absolutely invariable rules for special departments of human conduct. Goodness and Knowledge and the contemplation of Beauty and Purity and Love, these, we may say, are elements of the supremely good life: these are ends in themselves as well as—much more than pleasure; or, in popular language, we may say (if we please) that the pleasures resulting from these things are intrinsically higher or worthier than the pleasures attending upon mere animal satisfaction. And yet we feel that the intuitions on which such judgments rest can never be accurately defined or exhaustively set forth in words at all. Any attempt to do so would undoubtedly be merely provisional and temporary: it would necessarily be limited by the limitations and coloured by the idiosyncrasies of a particular time or a particular

* Prof. T. H. GREEN.

school, it may be of a particular nation or a particular class.

Take, for instance, the proposition, "Beauty is Good." I know that the attempt to apply any but purely artistic canons to the judgment of Art will be violently resented in some quarters. And so long as the judgment is purely æsthetic, I will not dispute the justice of the protest. But the moment we pass from the judgment "this is beautiful" to the judgment "this beauty is good to contemplate," or "this work of Art was right for man to create," we pass from the æsthetic region to the moral. And as a matter of fact, in actual practice, æsthetic criticism is seldom or never purely æsthetic. At least where the subject-matter of the Art is human life and character, the Artist's view of them and the judgment which the critic pronounces upon that view are always more or less coloured by his own ideal. In the most realistic Art there is some selection, and there is some suggestion; and the selection and the suggestion must both of them be governed by some kind of ideal. There is, then, a morally ennobling Art, and there is an Art that is not ennobling. And yet how difficult, how impossible the attempt to define in words the difference between the two in a way that should be valid for all time, that should enable future generations to discriminate between the good and the evil in artistic schools or ideals that are yet undreamed of! And still more impossible is the attempt to define in words the relative worth of the different elements which together make up the ideal life for the individual and for societies. Charity is good, and the pursuit of knowledge is good, and the contemplation of beauty is good; hatred of sin is good, and love of the sinner is good; meekness is good, and personal dignity is good. But how to express the due and proper relation between these various elements of our ideal? Here, even more than in the attempt to define the rule of conduct prescribed by particular virtues, we must recognise the truth of the principle—"Morality is internal," "the letter killeth." The true ideal of human life can never be adequately set forth in formulæ, though I believe that tentative and progressive attempts at the scientific analysis of our ideals are of the greatest possible value. The living character alone can fully express them: "the spirit giveth life." The man who loves his neighbour as he should, and who hates sin as he should, he and he only can prescribe the attitude which, under such and such particular circumstances, in this or that particular state of society—the mutual relations of the persons in question being what they are—should be adopted towards this or that wrong-doer. And it is the living character alone that can adequately teach the lesson to others. "Virtue *can* be taught, but in this way," as the author of *Ecce Homo* has put it, "by personal influence."*

These considerations may, I trust, help us to understand the real meaning of the term revelation when applied to the work and the nature of Christ. The moral ideal, and consequently the nature of God, have been revealed to us in the only way in

* *Ecce Homo*, chap. ix.

which any true and permanent revelation could possibly be made—in a perfect human character.

There are, indeed, ways of looking at revelation which are undoubtedly open to all the objections that have ever been urged against the idea. All attempts at finding a full and perfect expression of the moral law, or even of any section of it, in a mere series of propositions taken by themselves must necessarily be either inadequate or false. If the propositions are wide and general, they are inadequate. If they are particular and detailed, they can never be wholly or exactly true, whether the propositions be looked for in an infallible book, or in the utterances of infallible councils of fallible men, or in some infallible catena of authorities which learned men may laboriously construct from some ill-defined corpus of ancient writers. Even the utterances of Christ Himself, though we do well to attribute to them an authority which we can ascribe to no other human words, can only be regarded as a full and permanently valid expression of human duty when taken in their due relation with one another—with the circumstances of the time, and with all the words and acts which set forth for us the essential character of the speaker. Even of the words of Christ Himself, nay, of them more than of any other words, St. Paul's saying holds good: "The letter killeth, the spirit giveth life." Even that new commandment in which he summed up the law of his Kingdom would have been nothing but a quotation from one of the least spiritual books of the Old Testament,* apart

* Leviticus xix. 18.

from the parables and the example which gave a new answer to the question, "Who is my neighbour?" The love of that neighbour again becomes a wholly different thing according as we interpret our neighbour's needs by the teaching of Christ, or by the teaching of Epicurus and Bentham. And when we come to the more detailed precepts, how pitiful have been the caricatures of Christ's teaching that have resulted from every attempt to apply them to the circumstances of successive ages, after the fashion in which a judge applies an Act of Parliament! Of the sayings of Christ, no less than of the infallible intuitions of certain philosophers, it may surely be said that there is hardly one of them that, under certain circumstances, might not lead us wrong so long as we interpret it in the spirit of the mere lawyer or the mere casuist or the mere exegete. If we interpret them literally, we shall become old-fashioned Quakers or anti-social ascetics or unspiritual ceremonialists. And if we interpret them not literally, nothing but a grasp upon the character of Christ as a whole, nothing but a drinking in of the spirit of Christ Himself, can save us from explaining them away altogether. Nothing but the spirit of Christ can teach us when to see metaphor or paradox in His teaching, and when to see literal command, or how to penetrate beneath the metaphor or the paradox of the eternal truth which it was meant to teach.*

---

* Cardinal Newman has contended that apart from the judgment of the Church there is nothing to tell us that the feet-washing was not intended to be as permanent an institution of Christianity as the Eucharist. (*Prophetical Office of the Church*, 1837, Lecture xii. p. 334.) He is right, if only the Church be taken to mean the conscience of the whole Christian Society.

For no literalist is ever literalist at all points. Those who have attempted to be most literal in Ethics have often been most latitudinarian in all that relates to the Church or the sacraments; and those who are most literal as to the Church and the sacraments have often either been latitudinarian in their interpretation of the Sermon on the Mount, or have introduced a double standard of Ethics, one for the secular and another for the monk, a principle which might easily be shown to run as violently counter to the letter of Christ's teaching as it does to its spirit. Every utterance of Christ that has come down to us is infinitely precious as helping us to grasp the character which inspired it, and the character which it consequently enjoins upon us. Every result of criticism that can enable us, even in the minutest details, to get behind the small conflicts of the Gospel-narratives with more and more confidence to what we can be sure Christ really taught and really did, has its work to do in clearing up that historic picture of the Master, through which alone our generation can penetrate to the eternally valid laws of character which He has revealed. But let us ever remember that it is the *character* that is the abiding revelation both of God and of human life—that alone supplies an eternally valid "ethical criterion." Rules of conduct require to be interpreted, restricted, or developed in accordance with the changing needs of successive ages, and the inexhaustible variety of human circumstances. Even the revelation which Christ gave us, or rather the revelation which Christ Himself eternally *is* for us, would not be complete (as he Himself taught) without another revelation—the revelation of the Spirit. Whether any new development or proposed rule of conduct can or cannot be recognised by the Christian conscience depends, not so much upon the question whether or not it can be actually extracted from the recorded words of Christ, as upon the question whether it really flows from the principle of that teaching, whether we can suppose that in the present state of human society and human knowledge it would have been welcomed and acknowledged by Christ, or such as Christ. That it is no easy task to make this discrimination is undoubtedly true; and no mechanical system can ever make it otherwise than difficult. "For who among men knoweth the things of a man, save the spirit of man which is within him?" Only the spirit of Christ can recognise the Spirit of Christ. Only in so far as there is in our own hearts some measure of that Spirit which proceeds from the Father and the Son shall we be able to recognise the work which that Spirit is doing in the moral and religious, the social and intellectual movements of the society in which we dwell. The relation between the one revelation once made in the person and character of Jesus Christ and the ever-present progressive revelation of the indwelling Spirit to the individual and to the Christian Church or society opens up too large a subject to be further pursued just now. Suffice it for to-day to have pointed out that it is impossible to acquiesce in any attempt to condense into all-sufficient formulæ, or propositions, the teaching contained in either of these two revelations —in the eternal message which is contained in the character of Jesus Christ, or in what the Spirit is saying unto the Churches in each successive age.

The principle which we have been considering is not, I think, without a bearing upon certain questions of present-day controversy. We are rapidly outliving the old mistake of substituting the Bible for Christ, and again of supposing that revelation ends abruptly with the close of the New Testament Canon. Everyone to whom the work of God's Holy Spirit has not become either a piece of far-off history or a piece of far-off fable must sympathise with the revived belief in the Christian society as the medium of a continuous and progressive revelation to the hearts of men, a revelation never superseding, but always bringing out fresh depths of meaning in the one historic life of Him to whom the Spirit was given without measure. So long as we do not acquiesce in too narrow a view of the limits of this society, or too mechanical a view of the organs through which its true mind is declared, it must surely be admitted that the revived belief in the Church represents an advance, both spiritual and intellectual, for which we cannot be too thankful, either to the theological teachers with whom it originated, or to those social movements which are bringing it home to us to-day in another form. But along with this change has there not sometimes gone a tendency to substitute a mechanical exaltation of the letter of the Church's Creeds for a mechanical insistence upon the letter of the Old and New Testaments? That Christ is the only-begotten, the unique Son of God, is undoubtedly a great and precious truth, and it is natural and right that we should in worship and in education express this faith of ours in the language which the authority of the ancient Church has handed down to us. But let us remark that taken by itself this belief would have no moral value or significance whatever. It declares merely the fact that God has been revealed in the historical Christ and the society which he founded. That is a truth of infinite moment: to keep it ever present to our minds is, I suppose, the great use of the constant recitation of the Creeds in worship. But at the same time it is a truth which would be of very little spiritual importance to anyone who knew nothing as to what God has been revealed to be. Neither the Apostles' Creed nor the Nicene Creed contains the whole of the Christian Revelation. But for one fact, we might go so far as to say that the Creeds, taken by themselves, contain no revelation of God at all. We cannot say that, because in those opening words of both the ancient Creeds of Christendom, "I believe in God the Father," we do indeed find expressed the very heart of the Christian Revelation. But the mere use of that one word Father, which (in however different a sense) might be paralleled out of pagan Theology, could convey no real information or instruction to one who had not learned from the records of Christ's words and works what sort of Being they have shown God to be. Taken by themselves, the Creeds do not teach the supreme truth that God is Love, though interpreted by the Gospel records they do teach it. Even the Resurrection would mean very little to us apart from the character of Him who rose, or rather perhaps we ought to say, that belief in the Resurrection of Christ would not be a spiritual belief at all apart from teaching which the Creeds do not themselves contain, as to the nature of that future life to which the manifestation of the risen Lord bears witness. Hence it seems to me that to make the degree of a man's attachment to these ancient formulæ, however venerable, the one only test of his adhesion to the Christian Faith—to make their use in schools the sole test as to whether an education is Christian or otherwise—shows at the best a defective sense of proportion; and at the worst (I fear) a total failure to comprehend the very nature of that revelation of a divine life in man to which it is the object of the Creeds to testify.

It may be allowed that there is some pedantry and some sectarianism in the attempt to exclude the Creed from the Board Schools on the ground that it is a "denominational formula," but that cannot justify the use of wild language about Christianity having been banished from the schools. So long as the teacher teaches Christ's life of love, so long as he teaches that that life reveals to us the life of the Eternal Father, he does teach Christianity, he does teach the essence of the Catholic Faith. And let us remember also that where the teacher, whether in Board School or Church School, fails to bring home to the children's minds what sort of character was Christ's, and how they can become like Him, *there* will be no teaching of Christianity at all, though there be never so much recitation of Creeds, never so accurate an acquaintance with historical facts or doctrinal technicalities. We cannot teach anything whatever about God without a doctrine, and doctrines may for many purposes conveniently be condensed into formulæ. It is, therefore, impossible to sympathise with much of the current talk about an undogmatic Christianity. But to say that the formulæ cannot fully exhibit the most fundamental thing in Christianity—that is to say, the character of God as revealed in Christ, to say that formulæ often repel where the doctrine which they stand for would attract—is no more to cast a reflection upon their usefulness in their proper place than we reflect upon the value of ethical precepts by saying that they can never be more than very inadequate embodiments of the Moral Ideal, or that the highest ethical teaching can never be given by formal instruction in Morality. God and Duty alike can be adequately revealed in one way only—by a character, a life, a Personality.

VIII.

THE ABELARDIAN DOCTRINE OF THE ATONEMENT

Preached before the University of Oxford, at St. Mary's, 1892.

"Even as the Son of man came not to be ministered unto, but to minister, and to give his life a ransom for many."—MATTHEW xx. 28.

AMONG all the passages of the New Testament in which our Lord is said to have died *for* men, this is the only one in which the preposition ἀντὶ is employed.* The usual preposition is ὑπὲρ; and, where that is the case, I need hardly say that the attempt to read into the text the meaning "instead of," "as a substitute for," or the like, is wholly gratuitous. To suffer death, vicariously as a substitute for others, would no doubt be to suffer ὑπὲρ,† on behalf of, for the sake of others; but that is clearly not implied by the Greek. Christ may be no less truly said to have suffered on our behalf in

* With the parallel, Mark x. 45. It is possible that Luke xxii. 27 may be nearer to the original form of our Lord's saying. But even if a touch of theological reflection has been imparted to this record of our Lord's words, the tradition is clearly a very ancient one.

† Cf. the late Prof. Evans' note on ὑπὲρ in the *Speakers' Commentary, N.T.*, vol. iii. p. 371.

THE ATONEMENT

whatever way or ways his sufferings have tended to the benefit of his brethren still on earth.

When we come to the solitary passage from which my text is taken, the patristic idea of a satisfaction or propitiation and the more characteristically Protestant idea of a vicarious punishment, have at first sight more to say for themselves. 'Αντὶ undoubtedly does mean "instead of," "in place of." But a moment's candid consideration of the context will perhaps satisfy us that no theory of substitution can really get much support from the metaphor of our text. In the first place be it observed that even in this passage—the very *locus classicus* for such theories—the death of Christ is primarily set before us as an *example*: his death is looked upon as the culminating act of a self-sacrificing *life*. We are enjoined to serve our fellow-men in the same way in which Christ served us. The giving of His life is mentioned as the most signal instance of His ministry to his fellow-men: "Whosoever would be first among you shall be your minister. Even as the Son of Man came not to be ministered unto, but to minister, and to give his life a ransom for many." It is clearly most agreeable to the context to suppose that His death is set forth as being serviceable to others in the same sort of way as His life of teaching and example and sympathy.

But it may be asked, "To whom is the ransom paid?" That, however, is a question to which no answer need be, and (as I venture to think) no answer ought to be, given. The idea of a ransom paid to the devil and the idea of a ransom paid to

God are alike entirely foreign to the context. The idea is not that of a debt undertaken, still less of a punishment submitted to instead of us, but of a ransom paid to win us back from slavery or captivity. Christ's death was the price, the cost of that deliverance; the ransom paid is the equivalent, not of our sins, but of us. We are not debtors, but captives, whom Christ has emancipated at the cost of His own life. Is the question asked, Emancipated from what? Here, again, there is nothing in the immediate context to supply an answer. But, if a categorical answer must be given, the whole tenour of Christ's teaching requires us to say, "Emancipated from sin"—not primarily from the punishment of sin, nor yet from the spirit of evil, but from sin itself. Even this interpretation is perhaps pressing the metaphor further than need be. We ought to interpret the passage rather in the light of that dominant idea of all the Master's teaching, the idea of a Kingdom of Heaven. The prominent thought is not what Christ delivered men from, but what He bought them for. He bought them for His kingdom, He made them subjects of His spiritual empire, at the cost of His own death. That is the ultimate purpose of all Christ's work, of which even the deliverance from the slavery of sin is but a negative and a subordinate aspect.

The history of the interpretation of this text is indeed a melancholy example of the theological tendency to make systems out of metaphors. The earliest Christian writers cannot be said to have a theory of the Atonement at all*: their language admits for the most part of whatever interpretation we can legitimately assign to the New Testament expressions upon which it is based. Irenæus is the first to suggest with any definiteness the idea of a ransom paid by Christ to Satan. Entirely free from the horrible idea of an angry and revengeful Father propitiated by a loving and merciful Son, Irenæus does hold that a ransom was owing to the Prince of Evil. By sin man had become the thrall of Satan. Satan had acquired rights over him. God wanted to recover His lost dominion over fallen man, to win him back to His love and His service. But "it became God" (says Irenæus) "to receive what He willed by persuasion and not by force, so that neither might justice be violated nor God's ancient creation perish."† "Christ compensated our disobedience in the matter of the tree by His obedience on the tree." The death of Christ was brought about by Satan's machinations; but, since He was innocent, Satan had no right to *His* life; so that now it became compatible with justice that man, over whom he *had* just dominion, should be set free from his sovereignty. Why Satan brought about Christ's death, why he consented to accept Christ's death as an equivalent for his dominion over mankind (and indeed many other difficulties

---

* Harnack has emphasised the remarkable fact that the characteristic ideas of the Epistle to the Romans—which moderns have often taken as the whole of St. Paul—made no impression at all on the mind of the early Church. The post-apostolic age did not understand that side of the Apostle's teaching, so it simply let it alone.

† *Adv. Hæres.*, v. 1, 15, 21.

which may naturally arise) Irenæus leaves unexplained. The system suggested by Irenæus is more fully elaborated by Origen. In Origen,* and still more clearly in later Fathers, it appears that Satan was deliberately deceived by God. He was somehow or other induced to believe that in bringing about the death of Christ he would get possession of His soul. But there he had over-reached himself; he found that there was one soul which could not be held in Hades. The very device by which he had hoped to complete his triumph became the means of his own ruin, and the whole body of his ancient subjects escaped his grasp.

Such, in brief outline, was the theory of the Atonement which on the whole held possession of Christian Theology throughout the patristic period. In saying this, however, I ought to add that the Atonement, at least the theoretical justification of the Atonement, is not a prominent feature of patristic teaching. To the Fathers, "as to the Church of all ages," says Mr. Oxenham, "it was not the Atonement but the Incarnation which was the centre of Christian faith as of Christian life."† And in their teaching about the Incarnation, many of them—especially of the Greek Fathers—do suggest much nobler and more rational answers to the question how Christ's life and sufferings really did make possible a new spiritual birth for humanity at large

---

* *In Matt.* tom. xiii. 8, 9; xvi. 8; *In Rom.* iii. 7; iv. 11; *Contra Celsum* viii. 44; cf. BIGG, *The Christian Platonists of Alexandria*, Oxford, 1893, p, 210 *sq.*

† *The Catholic Doctrine of the Atonement*, ed. 3, 1881, p. 166, a work to which I must acknowledge great obligations.

as well as for individual souls—answers by the side of which the theory of a ransom owed to Satan may well be deemed as superfluous, as it must to every modern mind seem arbitrary, childish, and immoral. But so it is. In that edifice of gold, silver, costly stones, wood, hay, stubble, which the Theologians of the first no less than of later ages have built upon the one foundation, we must be content to cherish and to reverence the more precious and permanent elements, while we abandon the more perishable to their inevitable decay.

I will not attempt to trace this marvellous theory through the various phases and modifications which it underwent during the more than eight centuries of its almost undisputed reign. By minds like Origen's we may indeed doubt whether it was ever accepted with the deadly literalness with which it was certainly understood by some of his followers.* I wish to call attention rather to the work of the great men to whom Christendom owes its emancipation from this grotesque absurdity. Among all the enormous services of Scholasticism to human progress none is greater than this; none supplies better evidence that in very many respects the scholastic age was intellectually in advance of the patristic. The

* I do not feel at all sure that Origen's own language is not meant to be more or less metaphorical. He never quite explains why the 'traditio' of Christ to Satan serves as a ransom for those who had become his slaves. Sometimes Origen seems to be very near Abelard. "Hoc ergo modo etiam Christus occidit inimicitiam in carne sua, cum morte suscepta exemplum dedit hominibus usque ad mortem resistere peccatum : et ita demum resoluta inimicitia in carne sua, reconciliavit per sanguinem suum homines Deo, eos duntaxat qui inviolatum reconciliationis fœdus ultra non peccando custodiunt. (In Rom. iv. 12.)

demolition of this time-honoured theory was effected principally by two men—one the most lovable of medieval saints, the other the greatest of medieval thinkers; one the herald and precursor, the other the actual father or creator of the Scholastic Theology.* The attack on the received Theology was begun by St. Anselm; the decisive victory was won by Abelard. Seldom, indeed, has a theological system crumbled to pieces so rapidly, so completely, and so irrevocably. Abelard's timid disciple, Peter the Lombard,† is the last important writer to maintain this theory of a ransom paid to Satan. And among all that crop of strange and terrible theories of the Atonement which sprang up at and after the Reformation, the old patristic view has (I believe) never been revived.

Neither of these great Schoolmen were mere destructives. They demolish the ransom theory only to clear the ground for a worthier and more reasonable view of God's dealings with mankind. Anselm's theory of the Atonement is familiar to all theological students. And at the present day it will probably be felt that, though free from the coarse grotesqueness of the older view, it is open to some of the same objections as its predecessor on the score both of Logic and of Morality. In the *Cur Deus Homo* the death of Christ still remains a debt owed, not indeed to the Evil One, but to

* Doubt had been suggested by John of Damascus. *De Fid. Orth.* iii. 27; but cf. iii. 19.

† *Sent.* iii. 19. But there are traces of Abelard in his explanation; *e.g.*, "Mors ergo Christi nos justificat, dum per eam charitas excitatur in cordibus nostris."

an abstract Justice, or rather perhaps to God Himself. Man had sinned. By sin, by failing to be what God intended him to be, man had robbed God of something which was His due. Man had thereby incurred to God a debt so great that nothing in the whole universe that was not God could be an adequate compensation to Him. It would not beseem the honour or the justice of God that He should forgive man's sin without demanding this satisfaction. Nothing which was not God would satisfy His claims; and yet the debt must be paid by man. Even the Word, who was God, could satisfy it only by becoming man; only so could He die, and by so doing pay God something which was more precious than that of which God had been robbed by the sin of man, and yet something which was not owing to Him *ex debito justitiæ*.

I will not dwell upon the obvious difficulties of this scheme, which exercised more influence over Wycliffe and the Reformers than over Anselm's immediate successors. I leave it without comment, and pass on to the very different theory which meets us in Abelard. "To us it appears,"* he says, "that our justification and reconciliation to God in the blood of Christ lies in this, that through the singular favour exhibited to us in the taking of our nature by His Son, and His perseverance even unto death in instructing us alike by word and by example, God bound us to Himself more fully than before by love; so that, kindled by so great a beneficence of divine favour, true charity fears no longer

* *Opera*, ed. COUSIN, 1859, ii. p. 207.

to endure anything for His sake. . . . Accordingly our redemption lies in that supreme love working in us * through the passion of Christ, which not only liberates us from the slavery of sin, but acquires for us the true liberty of the sons of God; so that henceforth we fulfil all duties rather from love than from fear of Him who showed to us so great favour than which none greater can be discovered; as He Himself testifieth, 'Greater love hath no man than this, that a man lay down his life for his friend.' Concerning this love, indeed, the Lord says in another place, 'I came to send fire on the earth, and what will I but that it be kindled?' For the propagation of this true liberty, therefore, it is that He declares Himself to have come."

Three points may be noticed in this Abelardian view of the Atonement:—

(1) There is no notion of vicarious punishment, and equally little of any vicarious expiation or satisfaction, or objectively valid sacrifice,† an idea which is indeed free from some of the coarse immorality of the idea of vicarious punishment, but is in principle somewhat difficult to distinguish from it.

(2) The atoning efficacy of Christ's work is not limited to His death. Christ's redeeming work is

---

* Or possibly "excited in us": "Redemptio itaque nostra est illa summa in nobis per passionem Christi dilectio."

† That Christ's life and death were in the truest and highest sense a sacrifice is a doctrine of the highest value, and is quite consistent with the view taken in these pages. But to develope this aspect of our Lord's work falls beyond the scope of this sermon. I have tried to suggest the true sense in Sermon x.

not on the one hand confined (in Socinian fashion) to teaching or even example, though it includes both; His love to man reveals in a unique way the love of the Heavenly Father, because He is in a unique sense the Son of God. But neither, on the other hand, is His atoning work limited to the crucifixion. The whole life of Christ, the whole revelation of God which is constituted by that life, excites the love of man, moves his gratitude, shows him what God would have him be, enables him to be in his imperfect way what Christ alone was perfectly, and so makes at-one-ment, restores between God and man the union which sin alone has destroyed.

And (3) it follows from this view of the Atonement that the justifying effect of Christ's work is a real effect, not a mere legal fiction. Christ's work really does make men better, instead of merely supplying the ground why they should be considered good or be excused the punishment of sin, without being really made any better than they were before.

Justification and sanctification become (to quote the learned Romanist Theologian whom I cited before) "different names for the same thing, according as it is viewed in its origin or its nature, except that, in ordinary language, justification is used for the initial act on the part of God in a process of which sanctification, in its fullest sense, is the gradually accomplished result; they stand to each other in the spiritual life as birth in the natural life to the gradual advance to maturity."*

* OXENHAM, *op. cit.* pp. 227-8.

Such was the doctrine that moved the unmeasured wrath of Abelard's great enemy, St. Bernard. And, be it observed, St. Bernard is as vehement against the negative as against the positive side of Abelard's doctrine. To the Abbot of Clairvaux the doctrine of the Atonement stands or falls with that theory of the ransom paid to the devil which Catholic Christendom was (little as Bernard imagined it) just on the point of throwing off. If so, the saintly Archbishop of Canterbury was as great a heretic as Abelard, though neither he nor St. Bernard seems to have been aware of the fact. But whatever may be thought on this point, it is indeed strange that such a man as St. Bernard should solemnly include in a list of Abelard's heresies, which he prepared for the information of the Pope, the statement, "I think, therefore, that the purpose and cause of the Incarnation was that He might illuminate the world by His wisdom, and excite it to the love of Himself." Such was one of the doctrines (so far as we can gather) which was solemnly condemned by a Pope and a Council. Inadequate some even of our modern Theologians might pronounce it. But what a host of authorities —patristic, scholastic, Anglican, Protestant—might be produced in its favour! From what Theologian, since Theology began, could you not extract some close parallel to this beautiful expression of the whole Gospel message, unless it be some rigid Lutheran? And even the most rigid Lutheran cannot always remain faithful to a scheme of justification in which love plays no part, in which the love of God outpoured on Calvary is not allowed to awaken any response in the human heart, lest perchance even the admission of man's capacity for gratitude, often the very last spark of the divine nature to forsake the breast of the vilest criminal —lest even this admission might be to concede too much to human merit, and to detract from that comfortable doctrine of the total depravity of that human nature which God created in His own likeness and after His own image. Nor would the name of St. Bernard himself be absent from the *catena* of Abelard's adherents. Raising the question whether God could have found any other means of redeeming fallen man besides the method of the Incarnation, he replies (against Anselm) that He could have done so, but "He preferred to do it at His own cost, that He might find no further occasion for that worst and most odious sin of ingratitude in man."*

All through the Christian ages it has been surely the love of God revealed in Christ which really has won the heart of man, and made the Christian doctrine of the Atonement a real instrument of moral improvement, however inadequate, monstrous, even revolting sometimes has been the intellectual embodiment which it has received either from formal Theology or from popular sentiment. Those whose theories have most tended to obscure the doctrine of divine love have yet felt its power. But let it not be supposed that on this account theological theories are matters of no importance. Nobody, perhaps,

* Serm. xi. *in Cant.*

ever felt the divine love more powerfully, or worked more energetically in the strength of it, than Luther; and yet if the love of Protestant Europe seems to have waxed in these latter days so very cold, that there is some excuse for the contempt which it has unfortunately become fashionable among ourselves to speak of continental Protestantism, it is largely owing to the paralysing influence of that formal divorce which Luther proclaimed between religion and morality in his theories of a faith which did not necessarily work by love.

"The purpose and cause of the Incarnation was this, that Christ should illumine the world by His wisdom and kindle it to the love of Himself."* At the present day this heresy of Abelard's would be welcomed as the very heart and essence of Christ's good news by Christians of almost every shade of ecclesiastical and theological opinion. In all modern statements of the doctrine this aspect of the Atonement as a revelation of divine love occupies the first place. We do indeed find modern Theologians setting up side by side of this clear and intelligible doctrine theories, on the one hand, of an objectively valid satisfaction or expiation; on the other, of a mystical retrospective participation by Christians in the sufferings of Christ. But I venture to say that when these theories come to be analysed and thought out, it will be found that they resolve themselves either into that notion of vicarious punishment which is now so heartily repudiated by nearly all Theo-

* ABELARD, *Opera*, ii. p. 767.

logians,* or into what is practically the Abelardian view. If satisfaction does not mean vicarious punishment, what can it mean, except that the suffering Christ removed the consequences of sin by making a new life possible without punishment? Or, if we are told that Christ offered an acceptable sacrifice to the Father, to what, if the idea of appeasing an offended Deity be rejected, can the sacrifice be conceived of as owing its acceptability or validity, except to its actual effects in awakening the love of Christ and of all good, and the hatred of all evil? In what other way can another's suffering, or even the man's own suffering, be conceived of as purging away sin? Or if, as with Dr. Dale, the prominent idea is that the Christian identifies himself with Christ in such wise that he can really be said to have shared in His expiatory sufferings,† what can this mean (in actual sober fact) but that love towards Him who suffered awakens a sorrow for sin which does the work of actual punishment in the contrite heart? After all, I cannot but feel that these modern theories of the Atonement are not very deeply held. When the Theologian is defending his own orthodoxy or writing formal theological treatises, then he feels bound, out of deference to tradition, to a system of Biblical exegesis, or to the authority of great names,

* By none more fully and frankly (among orthodox Theologians) than by Canon Mason, *The Faith of the Gospel*, chap. vi., most of whose language I could cordially adopt, though his attempts to read new meanings into old language are not always quite satisfying.

† *The Atonement*, ed. xi., 1888, p. 425 *sq*. This view appears in combination with theories which seem to me attenuations of the traditional views which Dr. Dale repudiates.

to repeat more or less of the old language, while he repudiates what will seem to most minds its natural meaning and its logical consequences. But when he leaves the cave of theological formulæ and comes down into the world to speak to the hearts and consciences of men, then we find it is usually of the character of God revealed in Christ that he speaks, of the love of Christ for man in life and in death, of the demand which that revelation makes for answering love, of the example of Christ, of the hope inspired by His Resurrection, of the assurance which all this work of Christ brings with it of forgiveness, renewal, and spiritual life for all mankind. It is of these things that the preacher elects by preference to speak, rather than of satisfaction or expiation or mystic identification.

The hold which what I may venture to call Abelard's view of the Atonement (though, as I have pointed out, it is Abelard's only because he extricated it from the confused and childish notions with which it had been associated)—the hold which this view has obtained over the Church of to-day can hardly be traced back through any direct historical succession to the influence of Abelard. Abelard did indeed shatter for ever the theory of a ransom paid to Satan: and the more refined theories of the Atonement maintained by the later Schoolmen bear witness to his influence. But still the Church did not at once accept Abelard's view in its simplicity and entirety. The Schoolmen who followed Abelard inherited his dialectical method, and something too of his spirit. To men like St. Bernard the *Summa*

Theologiæ of St. Thomas, with its full statement of objections and free discussion of difficulties, would have seemed as shocking an exhibition of human pride and intellectual self-sufficiency as the *Theologia* of Abelard. But Abelard's successors do not share his boldness, his penetrating keenness of intellectual vision, his uncompromising resolve that, while authority shall have its due weight, neither truth nor reason nor morality shall be sacrificed to it. Even from the slight specimen I have given you of Abelard's teaching you may possibly have been struck with the modernness of his tone. Abelard, in the twelfth century, seems to stretch out his hands to Maurice and Kingsley and Frederick Robertson in the nineteenth. At least, I know not where to look for the same spirit of reverent Christian Rationalism in the intervening ages, unless it be in the Cambridge Platonists.*

Abelard's doctrine of Redemption is not the only feature of his teaching that savours of the modern spirit. The task which Abelard set before himself is precisely the task to which the Church of our day is imperatively called. In Abelard's day the task was essayed—almost for the first time in the history of the Church—of reducing Christian teaching to the form of a systematic and coherent body of philosophical doctrine. The human mind was just awakening from a long slumber, and was insisting that the traditional faith of the Church should give

---

* The Abelardian doctrine was, however, held by William Law. This was the main cause of the rupture between Wesley, whom he had profoundly influenced, and himself.

an account of itself. The result of the effort inaugurated by Abelard was the scholastic Theology. The scholastic Theology in its developed form only partially reproduced the spirit of its parent, but still nothing betrays more unfailingly a lack of the historical spirit and the historical temper than a tone of undiscriminating contempt in speaking of the scholastic Philosophy and the scholastic Theology. It was a noble and stimulating idea surely that of a science of the highest generalisations, a science that should present the deposit of traditional and historical faith in its due relation to all other branches of knowledge, accepting and fusing into itself the highest and the truest that is known from whatever source of God, the World, and Man! Such an ideal is surely wanted in days when Theology is in some danger of sinking into the mere antiquarianism, or the mere literary criticism, which are, of course, among the most important of its bases and its instruments.

The new truth which now demands to be adjusted with the old truth is not the same as the new truth of the twelfth or the thirteenth century. Darwinism and historical criticism are to us what the awakening of dialectical activity was to Abelard, and the rediscovery of a lost Aristotle to Albert the Great and Thomas Aquinas. The restatement—let us say frankly the reconstruction—of Christian doctrine is the great intellectual task upon which the Church of our day is just entering, and with which it must go on boldly if Christianity is to retain its hold on the intellect as well as the sentiment and the social activities of our time. And, depend upon it, the Church that has lost its hold of the first will not long retain its control of the last. In that great task the reverent study of the past is an essential element. As an age awakens to new spiritual needs, it often finds that its wants have been to a great extent anticipated, though undoubtedly the old truth can only be rescued from oblivion by becoming something different from what it was before. No two ages can ever see exactly alike. In this reconstruction of Christian Theology, I am convinced that we have something to learn from the scholastic Theologians, and most of all perhaps from the first, the greatest, the most modern of them all. Partly for this reason —as an illustration of what we may learn from him— I have ventured to speak of Abelard's doctrine of the Atonement, but still more because I believe it to be as noble and as perspicuous a statement as can even yet be found of the faith which is still the life of Christendom.

IX.

JUSTIFICATION

Preached before the University of Oxford, at St. Mary's, 1895.

"Being justified freely by his grace through the redemption that is in Jesus Christ."—ROM. iii. 24.

IT has seldom happened that larger theological issues have turned on the interpretation of a word than those connected with the meaning of δικαιόω. The Greek fathers are not indeed unanimous or consistent in translating it to "declare just." But they seem to have recognised that as the obvious and normal meaning of the word. In Latin Christendom the word "justificare" naturally carried with it the sense "to make just," a fact which does much to account for the enormous development of the idea of "grace" in Western Theology. At the Reformation once again the differences between the Catholics and the Reformers turned largely upon the same question. The Reformers, inspired by their zeal for the Pauline Theology understood in the light of Renaissance scholarship, held that justification meant the "being counted or treated as righteous" by God. Justification was to them a sentence of acquittal, pronounced not in accordance with the facts of the case, not in consequence of any actual righteousness of man, but solely on account of the imputation to him of the merits of Christ. Faith was indeed the condition of this sentence of acquittal by God, but it did not in itself constitute any moral change on the part of the sinner, and any actual righteousness on his part must come from a distinct and subsequent act on the part of God, technically known as sanctification. The Catholics, on the other hand, declined to admit that God acquitted and treated as righteous men who were not really righteous at all. For them justification meant the actual making righteous. The atoning work of the Son was not the ground of an arbitrary judicial sentence on the part of the Father, but the means whereby God actually produced a moral change in the heart of man, and so made it possible for God to remit the penalties incurred by sin. Justification thus becomes merely the beginning of the process of which santification is the completion.

As a mere matter of exegesis, there can be little doubt that the Reformers were in the right; δικαιόω in St. Paul does actually mean to hold righteous, not to make righteous. So much must necessarily be conceded in the interests of sound scholarship and honest exegesis. But no considerations of scholarship or of exegesis can compel us to hold that St. Paul thought, or to follow him in thinking, that God counts people righteous without at the same time making them righteous. Or at least, if we insist that the declaring of the sinner righteous precedes the actually making righteous, we must say with Cardinal Newman, "Justification is the voice of the Lord designating us;—designating us *what we are not* at the time that he designates us; designating us *what we then begin to be.*" *

While, then, we must beware of attempting to read into St. Paul's language ideas which were foreign to him, we may gladly recognise that the Catholic doctrine of Justification is in certain aspects more in harmony with the demands of Reason and of Conscience than that of the Reformers.

There is, indeed, a sense in which we must admit that Reason and Conscience were on the side of the Reformers. In so far as "grace" or the power to do right was supposed to be mechanically conveyed to unconscious recipients by means of the sacraments, so long as it was treated as a quasi-physical fluid which flowed through wholly physical channels into human wills, then we can sympathise with the Protestant indignation against what they supposed to be the Catholic doctrine of Justification. How far that interpretation is a fair one I will not now enquire. The belief in sacramental magic is happily repudiated by those who adhere most closely to Catholic tradition among ourselves. But apart from this materialistic conception there is much in the Catholic doctrine of Justification which will certainly commend itself to those who wish to see Theology brought into harmony with morality and with common sense. That God should punish the innocent instead of the guilty, that he should acquit the guilty instead of the innocent, that he should arbitrarily punish some and acquit others on account of the presence or absence of a certain quality called

* *Lectures on Justification*, Lect. iii. § 3.

faith, which has in itself no connexion with any moral change—this is a doctrine which is certainly not St. Paul's, and which certainly cannot be ours. The ideas of vicarious punishment and imputed righteousness are surely essentially and irretrievably immoral. Not so the doctrines of vicarious suffering and infused or transmitted righteousness We should have to shut our eyes to all the facts of life if we were to deny that one man is often— nay, normally—made righteous by the sufferings of another, or the righteousness of another. Every child in whom some measure of Christian character has been implanted by the love of a Christian mother, every social outcast in whom the desire of higher things has been awakened by the self-denying sympathy of a pastor or a friend, every society which owes its moral health to the exertions and the sacrifices of those who have gone before and created its traditions—all these are witnesses to the truth of the Christian doctrine of grace. Nor are outward and visible symbols without their efficacy in making men righteous, or (if we choose to say so) in conferring grace. The flag that appeals to the eye, the tune that strikes on the ear, have been known to awaken the flagging enthusiasm of the soldier or the citizen as effectually as the spoken word or the living leader. The sacramental principle only becomes unintelligible when it is limited to a mechanical seven or a mechanical two. The name sacrament may or may not be confined to ordinances expressly founded by Christ Himself; but the sacramental principle must surely be extended far beyond the range of stereotyped ecclesiastical ordinances.* The sacraments are assuredly not the only material symbols or social institutions which do actually, as a matter of moral experience, "confer grace" or the power to become good.

In this, as in so many other matters, it is not so much by their assertions as by their limitations that Theologians have sometimes sinned against the light. And so with regard to that particular kind of grace which has been technically styled justifying grace. The doctrine of justification by faith in Christ only becomes false when it is isolated, instead of being regarded as the most stupendous instance of a great principle attested by all human history and all human experience — the principle that of all the forces that make men righteous personal influence is the strongest. Men are justified by Christ when Christ's influence makes them better men.

In St. Paul and in technical Theologies the word justification is, no doubt, confined to the beginning of the Christian life. To St. Paul, writing at a time when definite acceptance of Christ necessarily took place at one clearly-marked and tremendous crisis of a man's life, it was natural to draw a sharp distinction between the influence of Christ in the first moment of acceptance and the subsequent progressive influence which he calls sanctification. To us, who have for the most part begun to experience some at least of the benefits that have flowed from the life and death of Christ in earliest childhood (whatever crisis

* The Roman Church recognises "Sacramentalia" beyond the Seven Sacraments strictly so called.

or crises of more deliberate acceptance of Him may have come later), such a distinction becomes less natural or less absolute.

I fear that to some these technical phrases of Theology may have been rendered so repellent by the harshness of some of the old Theologies which were really believed, and the half-believed survivals of them, that even the effort to find out their meaning may be a weariness to flesh and spirit. But sometimes it may be that these technicalities—these ghosts of controversies all but extinct—whether they meet with languid acceptance or with indignant rejection, may really stand between the soul and a rational acceptance of eternal Christian truth. Let us then try to emphasise the fact that the essence of the Pauline doctrine of justification lies in its assertion of the supreme moral influence of the self-sacrificing life and death of Jesus Christ, and of that knowledge of the Father to which His recorded acts and words bear witness. Other lives and other characters have had some of this justifying effect on man, but none such as His. Sometimes you will find that people very much in earnest about the practical following of Christ are unwilling to assent to theoretical statements about the unique character of his work and personality. But put the question to them in a practical form. Ask them, "What actual human life has ever had any effect at all comparable to the life of Christ in taking away the sin of the world?" Ask them what historic character they can for a single moment imagine themselves, in the conduct of their own personal life, putting in the position which they are willing enough in practice to accord to Christ as a full and adequate embodiment for them of the highest moral ideal that they can conceive, as constituting by its inherent attractiveness the most adequate of all motives for moral aspiration, as supplying them with the highest idea that they can grasp of the character of God Himself. Put the question in this practical way, and most of the people I am contemplating will have no hesitation in answering, "We can assign this position to Christ, and we can assign it to none other." Or if some of them may feel a difficulty in denying that but for the actual course of history, or but for our imperfect knowledge of that history, it would not be impossible in the nature of things to suppose that there may have lived persons since Christ's time whose characters might, under other circumstances, conceivably have appealed to the world as His has done, they would at least be prepared to recognise that in actual history the nearer any personal influence seems to them to approach to a capacity for being made a substitute for the influence of Christ, it has only been in proportion as we are able to recognise in that person's character the image which had originally been stamped there by Christ Himself. The very attempt to place some other man on a level with Christ will thus be found to be in reality a fresh piece of homage to the Master. Practically, then, nearly all that is best in the modern world does accept, with more or less fulness and more or less intensity, the essence of the Christian doctrine of Justification through Christ. It would accept it more completely

JUSTIFICATION

perhaps and more intensely if it could only know and recognise that it was accepting it, and not imagine a greater gulf than there really is between this moral influence which is acknowledged and the theological proposition which excites so much suspicion. The best way of attaining to the clearer and stronger faith that we desire is to recognise and make the most of, and above all to act upon, the faith that we possess.

I do not mean to say that that peculiar influence of Christ which Theologians had described as justification can in its fullest extent be separated from the conviction of the divine mission and the divine nature of this Christ whose character appeals to us as the highest thing in human history. Apart from that conviction, the life and death of Christ could not produce the assurance of the love of God that they do bring with them when accompanied by this conviction. What I do venture to urge is that we should approach theological problems from this practical, or ethical, or experimental point of view. If we begin with asking what Christ has been to others, what He is or may be to us, we shall perhaps find that the best way of approaching the question what Christ is in Himself. Or, to put the matter in a more technical way, the acceptance of the Christian view of the office of Christ will form the basis of any true doctrine as to His Person. Recognise Him as in history and in personal experience the Messiah and Redeemer of men, and you will not find it difficult— if you believe in a living God at all—to recognise in Him the unique Son and Revealer of God. To those who believe in a divine will governing the course of human history, it cannot be thought a mere accident that one man and one only is the source of and fulfils our highest moral ideal—our ideal of God Himself.

This idea, that the Christian knowledge of God is based not upon speculative reasoning but upon the conviction wrought in the soul by personal experience of the moral effects of Christ's life, is the fundamental idea of the Theology of Ritschl. So far we may welcome the influence which Ritschl has exerted upon that portion of German Theology which is at once liberal and profoundly Christian. But there are other Ritschlian tendencies upon which we may perhaps be allowed to look with less entire sympathy.

(1) Firstly, it may be quite true that to some who have discovered by personal experience the full height and length and breadth of what Christ can be to the human soul, it becomes *practically* a matter of immediate certainty that in that historic personality God is revealed—though even in such minds there must (one would think) be some suppressed links of logical inference, however unanalysable. Or at least we may say that some measure of personal appreciation of the influence of Christ's work is a condition of any spiritually valuable conviction of His unique position. But there is (it would seem) a tendency in the Ritschlian School to disparage the witness of Natural Theology or Philosophy to the existence of God and the witness which the existence of conscience bears even to the character of God. It is difficult to see how any revelation could possibly reveal God to

one who was not already at least predisposed to believe that there is a God to be revealed; or how, apart from the rational conviction that the highest in man must needs be the best representative of God's own nature, the profoundest insight into the moral supremacy of Christ's character, and the intensity of his religious consciousness, could make us accept that character and that consciousness as a revelation of God. However much we may value Ritschl's attempt to rest the claims of Christianity upon purely spiritual grounds, we must not let impatience of the theoretical difficulties of rational Theology hurry us into substituting a more intellectual Pietism for a rational faith.

(2) And secondly—what is really very much the same criticism from another point of view—it is surely a mistake to isolate the influence of Christ from the general moral experience of the world. Granted that the difference between the influence of Christ upon the soul and the influence of any other character in history rises to a practical incommensurability, granted that for those who have experienced it in its highest intensity this influence of Christ has in it something *sui generis*, unanalysable, incommunicable, yet it is surely a mistake not to recognise that it has something in common with those personal influences, those other vicarious sufferings of man for man which it so greatly transcends. If one may judge from the recently translated and very interesting work of Hermann, *Communion with God*, there is a tendency in the Ritschlian School, if not in Ritschl himself, to repeat the mistake of the

narrowest dogmatism by disparaging all moral teaching, and all moral influences before and other than the life of Christ. We must not deny that God has spoken to men at divers times and in divers manners to the fathers, though we are right in asserting the immense superiority of the light which God has vouchsafed to us in His Son. And it is a still more disastrous mistake to disparage what may be called the lower levels of Christian experience—the lower, the more obvious, the more easily intelligible of the effects of Christ and His work upon individuals and upon societies. Tell a man earnestly enquiring for spiritual light amid the practical difficulties and the theoretical perplexities of modern life, " If only you had the spiritual intuition of a St. Francis or a Luther, then you would see how the knowledge of Christ will lead you to a clear vision of God which will make you indifferent alike to ecclesiastical dogmas and to philosophical objections. But till you have that, you are no Christian; you will gain nothing either from accepting the Church's teaching about Christ or from your well-meant efforts to obey what you can understand of Christ's moral teaching and to imitate His example." Language like that, whether it proceed from medieval mystic or from old puritan or from enlightened Ritschlian Theologian, is but too apt to break the bruised reed and quench the smoking flax of humble Christian endeavour. Nor is teaching of that kind without its dangers even for those who can with real sincerity claim as their own some of this higher Christian experience to which the appeal is made. Antinomianism is the nemesis that awaits all religion which forgets that the acceptance of Christ is an activity of the same rational self which expresses itself also in the most elementary act of duty.

Let us then set no technical or arbitrary limits to justifying grace or to the saving efficacy which flows from the cross of Christ. Even those who have known little of conscious effort to follow Christ may not be wholly strangers to His saving work through their union with the society which Christ has redeemed. Let no one think that he is wholly outside the Kingdom which the Christ has founded because he cannot honestly feel that personal faith in Christ has been the main source of whatever good there is in him. No man who has ever breathed a Christian atmosphere, and tried to live up to the highest moral ideal that a Christian society sets before him, need think himself wholly alien to the Christian commonwealth. The best that is in him he owes to Christ. If he has ever allowed himself to be affected by the influences of a Christian home, if he has been fired by the example of a Christian character, if he has ever shrunk from what Christ taught the world to regard as sin, he has already experienced something of justifying grace. Let him not indeed be content with submitting himself to these indirect Christian influences. The Church has surely been right in recognising as Christian, as within its own pale, the infant who for many years to come will know nothing of Christ but what it sees reflected in a mother's love, or the immature Christian whose Christianity consists in little but reverent submission to the most positive precepts of Christian morality, and the positive ordinances of the Christian society. Normally and naturally, under the conditions of modern life, the indirect Christian influence precedes the direct.* The Church is not a close oligarchy of perfected or mature Christian men, but a great educational institution in which men are gradually brought ever more and more completely and effectually and directly within the circle of Christ's influence. The abuse of ecclesiastical Christianity begins when the mere formal Church membership or the punctilious external performance of Christian ordinances is taken as a substitute for the moral effort which they are meant to assist.

But there is an opposite danger which is probably in these days far more widely spread. In many minds which are far enough from definite acceptance of any particular doctrine of Justification, the popular Protestant ideas about the Atonement have probably left behind them just this much—a disposition to believe that Christ's death has done some great but vaguely-conceived thing for us which saves us the trouble of doing anything for our own salvation. Now if there be any truth in the view that Justification may practically be treated as equivalent to the influence of Christ, it is clear that we cannot expect to be redeemed by a life and a death of which we never think. Indirect Christian influences should

---

* There is an admirable defence of Infant-Baptism on these lines in Canon Curtis' Bampton Lectures, *Dissent in its Relation to the Church of England*, Lect. iv.

JUSTIFICATION

of course lead up to, and prepare the way for, the more direct and personal influence of Christ. The capacity for appropriating (so to speak) the spiritual influence contained in the records of Christ's life varies (let us admit it) in different persons. Still, some help and instruction and inspiration it is possible for all of us to obtain from thinking about Christ: and some power there is in all of us of cultivating whatever spiritual capacity of this kind we possess. But we are not likely to think much about Christ unless we have regular times for thinking about him and for directing our wills towards him. Perhaps the uses of Christian worship would be more valued among us, and especially the uses of frequent and regular attendance at Holy Communion, if we thought of these ordinances more frequently in this simple light as so many definite opportunities for thinking about Christ, and trying to bring His influence to bear upon our lives.

And I will venture on one other very plain practical suggestion. I believe that a little intellectual study of the Gospel records—the intellectual effort to construct for ourselves (not without help from modern theological scholarship) some historical picture of Christ's life and to get an intellectual grasp of the central ideas of his teaching, I believe intellectual work of this kind would have more distinctly spiritual value than is often supposed. We cannot help being more or less affected by the destructive influences around us, the vague scepticism and unrest by which we are surrounded. Intellectual as well as moral effort is needed to counteract them. There are not many people of any seriousness of character who do not feel that they could wish that they were more influenced by Christ and His teaching than they are. Do they ever ask themselves what they have done, what they are doing to secure more of this influence, to give this influence the opportunity, so to speak, of finding its way into their soul? Doubtless the most important of all conditions for securing deeper spiritual insight is the effort to live up to the light we have. If any man will do His will, he shall know of the doctrine. The more he does, the more he will know. But still it is true also that faith cometh by hearing, and hearing is a voluntary exercise of the intellect. If it does no more, the mere occupation of the intellect about the life and the ideas of Christ might often draw fresh virtue out of words which have become impotent for us through sheer unintelligent, unreflecting familiarity with their sound. The Bible can never be to us just what it was to our fathers. It may be to us something more, but for that to be we must understand it better.

But in all this it may be thought I have been evading the chief point of St. Paul's teaching about Justification. Granted that all these moral influences flow from the work of Christ, it may be said, you have left out all account of the most characteristic influence of all. In all other respects no doubt we may trace an analogy between the influence of Christ and the moral influences that flow from the influence of other heroic or saintly, though imperfect characters. But what light does all this throw upon the one distinctive influence which is claimed by the New

Testament and by all Christian Theology for the work of Jesus Christ, the forgiveness of sins, and the assurance of that forgiveness which the acceptance of Christ carries with it. This is a vast subject on which much might be said, but I must be brief. Undoubtedly the conviction that God has spoken to us through His Son does convey to the believer an assurance of the forgiveness of sins. "Justification is simply forgiveness," it has been said by the latest Commentators on the Epistle to the Romans.* St. Paul's teaching about Justification is really after all the teaching of our Lord Himself in the parable of the Prodigal Son. And by that pregnant word more light has been thrown upon St. Paul's inmost meaning than is to be got out of whole libraries of dogmatic Theology. But after all even forgiveness is not so simple an idea. The idea of forgiveness stands almost as much in need of explanation as the idea of Justification. To the souls awakened to the sense of sin, and doubting if it were possible for such as they to obtain acceptance with God, the idea of the crucified Son of God hanging upon the cross for them has no doubt brought an assurance of forgiveness to which no explanation could add and from which no analysis could take away. But if we are to have Theology, we must have explanation. And may not the refusal to think spring from intellectual sloth or intellectual cowardice as often as from genuine humility? Is not the most inadequate attempt at explanation more reverent than the dogmatic assertion of the unintelligible? And

* SANDAY and HEADLAM, p. 36.

here perhaps the Commentators' reference to the Master's own teaching in the parable of the Prodigal Son may carry us some way towards a solution of our difficulty. It encourages us at least to appeal to human experience and ordinary human moral ideas in our thoughts about God's dealings with man. When, then let us ask, does a good father or a good ruler forgive and why? On what principles does he decide when he ought to forgive, when to punish? Surely he looks to the true good of the child or the subject with whom he has to deal. So far as the influences of the precedent upon others will allow him to do so, he will forgive just when and so far as the true good of the son or the subject will be better promoted by forgiveness than by punishment. If in remitting a penalty he may be said to count the unjust just, he only counts just that he may make just, exactly as he only punishes that he may make just. And it is a matter of common human experience that there are times and circumstances when forgiveness—the exhibition of love, especially when the forgiveness and the proffered love involve self-sacrifice—touches the heart and awakens the higher nature more powerfully than any punishment or exhibition of anger could do. Fully then may we grant that Justification, in its strictest Pauline sense, means the proclamation of forgiveness to the repentant sinner. But at the same time we must assert emphatically that Catholic Theology is not substantially wrong when it declares that Justification means making the sinner righteous. For only in so far as forgiveness will make the sinner better can we reverently attribute forgiveness to God. Indeed the proclamation of forgiveness can hardly be separated from the idea of the love that inspires forgiveness. The love that forgives can hardly be distinguished from the love that it makes us better to know. Forgiveness and punishment alike (though both forgiveness and punishment are no doubt inadequate expressions for God's righteous dealings with human souls) must surely be regarded as flowing from the changeless love of God which was most signally revealed in the life and death of Christ, and which—just because it was revealed—cannot be considered to have been for the first time brought into being when the Son of God died upon the cross.

X.

THE IDEA OF SACRIFICE

Preached in the University Chapel, Aberdeen, January 16, 1898.

"For the bodies of those beasts, whose blood is brought into the sanctuary by the high priest for sin, are burnt without the camp.
"Wherefore Jesus also, that he might sanctify the people with his own blood, suffered without the gate."—HEBREWS xiii. 11, 12.

THERE has been much controversy of late as to the origin of sacrifice, and (when we are dealing with primitive society) that is much the same question as the origin of Religion. It has been too hastily assumed in some quarters that the original idea of sacrifice was propitiation—a view which carries with it the theory that the origin of Religion is to be sought in selfish terror. According to this view, sacrifice is at the best a present to avert the wrath of a deity whose favour can be bought only by food and drink; at the worst a sop to a cruel monster delighting in blood for the sake of blood. But the more careful researches of men like the late Professor Robertson Smith* have shown that the idea of the

---

* *The Religion of the Semites* (New Edition, 1894), p. 214 *seq*. The same views are developed by Dr. F. B. JEVONS in his admirable *History of Religion*.

sacrifice as a present, and still more of the sacrifice as expiation, are comparatively late after-growths upon the original conception. The original notion of the sacrifice was the common meal in which the members of a clan or tribe entered into or ratified their union with the friendly tribal deity, and also with one another, by mixing with their own blood the blood of the Totem-animal—of the animal from which the tribe was supposed to be sprung, and which was in some sense identical with or representative of the tribal god. The rite of sacrifice is thus connected on the one hand with the idea of the blood-covenant by which, through the shedding and interchange of blood, an artificial union is established between those who are not of kindred stock by nature, and on the other with the natural and universal symbolism of the family meal. In a word, the primitive idea of sacrifice was not so much propitiation or expiation as communion.

It would of course be fanciful to credit the author of the Epistle to the Hebrews with any anticipation of these anthropological views about the origin of sacrifice, but the light which modern investigations have thrown upon the sacrificial idea will, I think, really help us to enter into the writer's attitude towards sacrifice. There is no book of the New Testament which is so full of sacrificial language as the Epistle to the Hebrews. Its author has contributed more perhaps than even St. Paul or St. Peter to fix and stereotype the idea of sacrifice in connexion with the death of Christ.

And yet it would, I think, be easy to show that

many of the theories that have grown out of his teaching are the very opposite to what he intended. To understand him, we must think ourselves back into the mental atmosphere of a world in which the idea of religion was inseparable from the idea of sacrifice. He was labouring to persuade Jewish Christians that for them the sacrificial system of the old world ought to be regarded as a thing of the past. To effect his purpose he had to put himself at their point of view, to assume (with them) that sacrifice was somehow essential to the wiping away of sin. And therefore he tries by every subtlety of interpretation known to Alexandrian Judaism to show that the old sacrifices had been types of a true sacrifice yet to come, the one all-sufficient sacrifice which had been offered by Jesus the Messiah in His death upon the cross. It is not necessary to suppose that he analysed very precisely in what sense sacrifice was necessary to take away sin. He was content to acquiescence in the ordinary Jewish point of view. His argument is largely an *argumentum ad hominem*. But, though he uses the language of the sacrificial theory, you will find, I think, how constantly he is trying to substitute higher and more spiritual ideas for the crude notions of his readers about the atoning efficacy of blood; and very often (to say the least of it) he does this simply by going back to the primitive idea of communion and trying to separate it from the later and lower idea of expiation. It was not possible, he tells his readers, for the blood of bulls and of goats to take away sin. There at once he destroys the whole idea of expiation in its

THE IDEA OF SACRIFICE

literal, materialistic form. The blood of Jesus would have been equally powerless so long as it was looked upon merely in the same light as the old sacrifice, merely as the offering of a very precious thing to an angry god, or as a piece of mere magic which in some wholly non-moral and non-spiritual way was to remove the stain of guilt. But, constantly as he uses the language of ritual sacrifice so natural to himself and to his readers, that language does not express his deepest thought about the matter. For him it was not the physical death, but the perfect obedience of Christ which gave that sacrifice its atoning value.

" Sacrifice and offering thou wouldest not . . . . in burnt offerings and sacrifice of sin thou hast no pleasure" (so the writer quotes one of the most anti-ritualistic utterances in the Old Testament), "Then said I, Lo, I come, in the volume of the book it is written of me, that I should do Thy Will, O my God." Obedience to the Will of God is the only true sacrifice! Half of the crudeness of the old Atonement doctrines would be gone if that had been always remembered. Although he does speak in the symbolic language which his hearers would appreciate of the new covenant between God and the spiritual Israel as ratified by the blood of His Son, he is always trying to lead their minds up from the merely physical to the moral aspect of sacrifice. The essence of the new covenant was not a physical participation in blood but a union of wills. "This is the covenant that I will make with the house of Israel after those days, saith the Lord; I will put my laws into their mind, and write them on their hearts; and I will be to them a God, and they shall be to me a people."*

We must remember too the illuminating remark of the present Bishop of Durham,† that to the Jewish mind blood suggested not the idea of death but the idea of life. In the blood is the life. That, as we have seen, is the idea which lay at the root of primitive sacrifice. Let us only think of the death of Christ — the crowning act in a whole life of sacrifice—as giving new life to the world, renewing its spiritual and moral being by a life of love such as had never been lived before and has not been lived since (in so far as it has been lived), without help from the virtue that has come out of that one life. Let us think of the death of Christ so, and we shall have no difficulty in giving a real, spiritual, present-day meaning to the idea of Christ's Atonement. By communicating His life to us Jesus Christ has verily and indeed taken away—is now verily and indeed, by no juridical fiction, but as a matter of actual human experience, taking away the sins of the whole world.

Or if we turn to the God-ward aspect of Christ's work, we may think of a sacrifice as that which establishes and makes possible communion between God and man. We shall see in that life of love the supreme self-revelation of God to Man—the love of God revealing itself in a human life and so awaken-

---

* Jer. xxxi. 33; Heb. viii. 8.
† WESTCOTT's *Epistles of St. John* (1883), p. 34, and *Epistle to the Hebrews* (1889), p. 293.

ing answering love in other souls and breaking down the sin which alone keeps God and man apart. By His life and death the Christ communicates to us too His own sense of Sonship, enabling us too to lead that life of Sonship which He had realized so perfectly. This surely gives a more real and a far higher sense to the New Testament doctrine that God was in Christ reconciling the world to Himself than we shall ever get at by any attenuation or refinement of the idea that Christ's sufferings and death were a punishment which God had sent the innocent Jesus to endure as the substitute or representative of guilty man.

And then observe how, immediately after the words of my text, the writer goes on to spiritualise and elevate the idea of worship as he had spiritualised the idea of Atonement. The spiritual sacrifice of the heart and the will is what the new covenant requires in the place of ritual oblation. The Christian Church has, indeed, "an altar whereof they have no right to eat who serve the tabernacle." The work of Christ, commemorated in the Christian Eucharist, is what enables us to offer more or less imperfectly the one true sacrifice—that sacrifice of the will which He once offered perfectly. "By him therefore let us offer the sacrifice of praise to God continually, that is, the fruit of our lips giving thanks to his name." And then (as he goes on to suggest) the sacrifice of the will in worship is but a means to the sacrifice of the life; communion with God must inspire and be realized in communion with our fellow-men. Almsgiving too—from the earliest times an essential element of every Eucharistic oblation—almsgiving too is sacrifice. "To do good and to distribute forget not, for with such sacrifices God is well pleased."

All through the history of Religion you will find a struggle between these two ideas of sacrifice—communion on the one hand, expiation on the other. We need not deny that there was a moral side to the craving for expiation—even when it showed itself in wild and savage and cruel rites—in so far as it testified to that sense of sin which, as the writer of our Epistle sees, such rites could never really take away. But still, it is broadly true, I think, that Religion has become higher or lower, its influence has been moralising or lowering, just in proportion as the idea of communion has predominated over that of propitiation or expiation. The religions of the old world, the most primitive cults, the crudest rituals were a beneficent and moralising influence just so far as they testified to a sense of communion between members of the same tribe or family and between the worshipper and the kindly, friendly tribal deity. They became non-moral or immoral in proportion as the idea of communion was supplanted or overlaid by the idea of propitiating a cruel or hostile deity who took pleasure in torture and in death. Here was the motive which inspired the old abominations of Moloch, or the hideous cult of Juju which has just been ended by the annexation of Benin to the British Empire. It is a comfort to be assured by Anthropologists that human sacrifice does not represent a universal primitive stage of Religion out of which humanity has but slowly and gradually emerged, but is merely a comparatively late and occasional degeneration from earlier and more healthful ideas and practices. I need not dwell on the manifold ways in which men's conception of God has at certain moments in the history of Christian thought been blackened by propitiatory theories of the Atonement. The Theology of Substitution is happily melting away before that representation of the Atonement as a revelation of the love of God which, though it has never been without a witness in Christian Theology, is associated especially with the teaching of Abelard and in modern times with that of Frederick Denison Maurice.

So, too, the idea and the influence of the Christian Eucharist has risen or fallen far as the idea of communion has or has not predominated over that of propitiation. There is no real antagonism between the idea of communion and the idea of sacrifice. Sacrifice at its highest *means* communion with God and our fellow-men. We may welcome heartily and unreservedly the modern tendency to emphasise the sacrificial character of the Church's Eucharist, if only we do not forget that the true sacrifice is the sacrifice of the will. The old liturgies are full of the idea of sacrifice, but then they assert with equal emphasis what their modern imitators sometimes forget, the contrast between the bloody sacrifices of the old covenant and the unbloody spiritual sacrifice, the reasonable sacrifice, the λογικὴ λατρεία of the new.

And this idea that sacrifice is communion is not without deep significance for practical morality. The idea of self-sacrifice does indeed represent the very heart of the Christian ideal of life. That a man finds his true life, his true self, in giving up the lower life for others—that is the very essence of the Gospel which Christ taught to the world by His life and by His death. But sometimes we find exaggerations, distortions even, of this purely ethical doctrine of self-sacrifice. Sometimes it is forgotten that the value of the Sacrifice depends upon the value of that for which lower goods are surrendered. "Sacrifice alone, bare and unrelieved," says Frederick Robertson, "is ghastly, unnatural, and dead; but self-sacrifice, illuminated by love, is warmth and life." The true self-sacrifice should be always a sacrifice of something lower for the love of something higher or for the love of other men.

There is no noble life without service, and the service of others always must involve some sacrifice of self—of things otherwise good and innocent for the sake of others. But we must not fall into the way of talking (there are few in our day who are tempted to such mistakes in practice) as if the ideal life allowed no enjoyment, in moderation and due subordination, of lower pleasures, and still less as if there could be no place in a Christian's life for Art or Literature or Science. Only we must not forget the one thing which can sanctify our enjoyment—its being shared with others. The old animal sacrifice, Pagan or Jewish, was not as a rule a giving up of the whole victim to the god, but rather a sharing it—with the deity and with his other worshippers. On us who believe that it is not some little circle of tribe or family that is linked to us by the tie of brotherhood, but the whole humanity whose sonship to God was proclaimed and made possible by Christ—on us this burden of communicating ought to weigh more heavily and yet more joyfully than on those who knew only the ties of blood or of class. Those who find most of their own joy in the joy of others come closest to the ideal of brotherhood. But still it would give us clearer ideas of social duty, I think, if we bore in mind that sacrifice is essentially sharing, not self-denial or self-mortification as such. It is not because pleasure and enjoyment are wrong or bad in themselves that a Christian conscience may find scruples about some of the amusements and indulgences which the world takes as a matter of course in the rich and well-to-do, but because pleasure and enjoyment are so good, and such vast numbers of our fellow-men get so little of them, and they might get so much more if rich men would spend less on big houses and smart carriages, on dinings and yachtings, or in enabling their sons to spend a great deal more money than is good for them in the Army or at the Universities. It is not because culture and intellectual life are unworthy of a Christian man's attention that the Christian will condemn a life of mere selfish dilettantism, and that even the student must sanctify his intellectual life (as he must sanctify all other enjoyments) by in some way or other sharing it with others. It is not because a highly cultivated class is not an invaluable element of social well-being that we pronounce the gospel of culture one-sided, but because others outside that class possess capacities for a higher life which can only be realized if those who possess culture will share it with those who have not. One need not be a believer in any mechanical equality or State Socialism to ask oneself anxiously sometimes whether we of the comfortable classes do not in some ways and directions get much more than our share of the good things of life. How much and in what direction each one of us might and ought to surrender some of these things for others, I must not now enquire.

On this matter as in others there are differences of vocation. Let us reverence those who are called to the higher and more exacting kinds of social service—those whose work may be described as missionary work, whether at home or abroad, whether of the directly religious order or in the numerous spheres of philanthropic and social work, which call for heroic sacrifices, essentially unpleasant services, great surrender of the ordinary comforts, recreations, and interests of cultivated life. And for all of us, in the most humdrum and conventional spheres of labour, the resolution to serve will certainly involve some sacrifice of pleasure and inclination, some endurance of hardness—at some crisis or other of our lives, probably, some more or less agonizing conflict with selfish inclinations. Do not think for one moment that I am trying to persuade myself or others that the service of Christ is a soft and easy thing. The Christian life would be a poor thing if it involved no sacrifice, and in all sacrifice there is pain. But after all, it is a mistake, and a ruinous mistake, to speak as if social service were essentially and necessarily unpleasant or uninteresting or inconsistent with the high development and enjoyable exercise of our highest capacities—as if self-sacrifice in one direction were not usually and normally compensated by a higher development of self in another. The work of every profession may be made into a branch of strenuous social service if it is really the opportunity of social service that we are looking out for, and not merely the pay and the reputation and the social position. Work does not always cease to be interesting when it ceases to be showy. A highly-educated man might find, for instance, in the work of local government and social reform in his own immediate neighbourhood as much exercise for the highest gifts of statesmanship or administration as a Cabinet Minister or the governor of an Indian province, if only his ambition be really to serve his country and not to win a ribbon or to pose as a personage in fashionable drawing-rooms. Others might find in the teaching of the poor a sphere for exactly the same faculties that are more remuneratively exercised in the teaching of the well-to-do. Medical work among the poor or the disinterested pursuit of Science is not surely less rich in intellectual interest than an aristocratic practice. Mere amusements again would not lose all their charm if pursued sometimes in the company of the poor who want nothing more than just to be taught how to amuse themselves rationally: and the society of a working-men's club would sometimes probably be found less boring than the society which men struggle most and squander most to enter.

But these are mere suggestions as to the way in which we ought to seek to apply, each for himself, the great law of sacrifice. Applications I must leave: all that I want to do here is just to enforce the principle—the principle that for the Christian the enjoyment of all good things must be sanctified by being in some way or other shared with others. For most of us, in practice, I think, the living out of that principle will mean not so much any eccentric asceticism, extreme hardship, or heroic self-renunciation, as a life of hard work, self-restraint, simplicity, moderation in living and in enjoyment, that we may have time and money, interest and energy left to help others enjoy too all that is best worth enjoyment in life—not so much surrender of privilege or position as a stronger sense of social duty and of the needs—material, intellectual, spiritual—of those less favoured classes of our fellow-men whom Christ taught us to call brothers.

True Sacrifice is Communion—that is the principle that we want to apply to our Theology, to our worship, but most of all to our practical and social life.

XI.

THE RESURRECTION AND IMMORTALITY

Preached before the University of Oxford, at St. Mary's, May 16, 1897.

"But as touching the dead, that they are raised; have ye not read in the book of Moses, in the place concerning the Bush, how God spake unto him, saying, I am the God of Abraham, the God of Isaac, and the God of Jacob? He is not the God of the dead, but of the living: ye do greatly err."—ST. MARK xii. 26. (R.V.)

AT times I imagine that some of us have been inclined, or would have been inclined, did reverence allow, to suspect something irrelevant or sophistical in these words of Christ. And yet, I think, a very little consideration will show that they really express, in a form adapted to Jewish ideas, the one great argument which has made most sincere believers in God believers in Immortality also. It was inconceivable, our Lord teaches, that a being who had once been deemed worthy to hold communion with the Eternal should really be the mere creature of a day, "coming up as a flower, cut down as the grass, never continuing in one stay." If God had ever really regarded with favour the traditional forefathers of the Jewish race, it was impossible that

that favour should be limited to the brief span of this earthly life. A being so honoured must surely be reserved for some higher destiny than a mere going down into silence. If God had indeed been their God unto death, must He not be their God even beyond death? Such was the line of thought—if we should not rather say the line of feeling—which had actually engendered in the more earnest and religious section of the Jewish race, between the age of the exile and the Christian era, what has been well described as "the greatest revolution which the human mind had ever experienced"—the revolution by which "man had come to consider or suspect himself to be immortal."* Such was the argument by which our Lord now meets the objections of the worldly, rationalistic, conservative Sadducean hierarchy. To Him no doubt the thought presented itself rather as a spiritual intuition than as a formal argument: but it is in principle the same argument which has made almost every thinker who has been in earnest about Theism a believer in Immortality also. The inadequacy of the present life to satisfy the demands of the moral consciousness, the aspiration of the human spirit not merely or chiefly for happiness but for knowledge and for holiness, the enormous contrast between the capacities with which human nature has been endowed and the meagre realization which can in general be given to them within the span of this earthly life, the energy with which Reason affirms that Justice ought to prevail in the affairs of men when contrasted with the equally

* *Ecce Homo*, chap. iv.

emphatic teaching of experience that Justice prevails not yet—these are the commonplaces of Christian Philosophy (amid however much more questionable argumentation) from the *anima naturaliter Christiana* of Plato down to the days of Kant and of Lotze. Surely when we find this reasoning sanctioned—in however different an outward dress—by Jesus Christ Himself, we may be allowed to question the wisdom of those who in His name have sought to disparage all arguments for Immortality except that which is based upon the historical evidence of His Resurrection. Beyond all doubt the tidings that mortal eyes had seen the Lord after that He had risen from the dead did, when taken in connexion with the rest of the Christian Gospel, produce an intensity of belief in a life beyond the grave which probably could have been developed by no other means. Beyond all doubt that simple tradition is even now capable of inspiring with spiritual hopes souls and lives that would be deaf to all our reasonings from the facts of the moral consciousness and the rationality of the Universe. But, for those who have once learned to look with critical eyes on the recorded narratives of wonderful events, the historical evidence of the Resurrection story will seldom bear *all* the weight of this momentous belief. For them assuredly what they think of the historic Resurrection will depend largely on what they have independently come to believe about God and Christ, about the meaning of human life and the destiny of the human soul. The evidence that the Apostles believed themselves to have seen the risen Lord is, indeed, evidence which no sober criticism can set aside: but each of us must inevitably interpret and explain that belief of theirs in accordance with his own presuppositions. I do not think that many of those who have accepted the faith that in a real sense Jesus Christ was the Son of God will permanently be content to look upon the appearance of the risen Jesus as a mere illusion, though they may demand more latitude than Theologians have sometimes allowed, in their theories—or perchance in their refusal to bind themselves by any theory—about the exact nature of the recorded appearances of the risen Lord.

We should not then disparage the clearness and the definiteness which is added to the Resurrection hope by the belief in Christ's risen and eternal life with God, symbolised and attested by the vision of the Apostles. Nor need we reject the support which may be given alike to the Resurrection of Christ and to the Resurrection of all men by sifted and well-attested evidence of more or less analogous appearances of the dead or the dying to their friends. But it is not wise unnecessarily to hazard so vital a part of the Christian Faith upon a particular answer to difficult historical, critical, or psychological problems. The evidence for the Resurrection vision is of a kind which can hardly appeal to those who are not already at least predisposed to the belief in human Immortality. Contact with critical problems inevitably awakens doubts and difficulties: and, however conservative our own solution of those problems may be, it is madness to tell people that unless they can give a particular answer to these critical and historical questions, they have no ground for believing in the Immortality of the Soul. It is better to say "we believe in Immortality because we believe in God; and because we believe in Immortality we find it possible to believe that the Son of God may have appeared to His disciples after that He was risen from the dead."

Undoubtedly the argument of our text does imply that one great presupposition—belief in God. In the form in which our Lord addressed it to His Sadducean opponents it assumes of course further that Abraham and Isaac and Jacob were special favourites of the God of Israel. For those who share Christ's own faith in God as the common Father, not merely of the Jewish nation but of the whole human brotherhood, the argument will have to be universalised. It is not merely Abraham and Isaac and Jacob, but the whole race of mankind—the race whose moral capacities have been illustrated by the saints and heroes of all time, and most of all by Him on whom Christendom looks as something more than saint or hero—it is that whole race of mankind that we cannot believe to have been destined by God for a life so poor and so meaningless as this life must needs seem to be for the vast majority, if it be not intended as the prelude and the education for something better. "Christ the first-fruits, afterwards they that are Christ's."

There are indeed just a few thinkers who, looking at the whole course of human affairs, are able to satisfy themselves by mere empiric evidence of the rationality of the world's history without any faith in Immortality. I confess I can only envy such men their philosophic optimism. I cannot but suspect that they sometimes forget that at most it is only to a Reason that sees the whole that the whole course of events can justify itself on the assumption that for each individual soul death ends all. Clearly there can be no *good* that is not enjoyed by some conscious spirit. And, if this life taken by itself is but a questionable good to so very many, it is difficult to see how the sum or the series of human lives, each of them individually unsatisfactory, can make up collectively a panorama on which the eye of reason can rest with any real satisfaction.

I do not mean for one moment to suggest that pain and sorrow in themselves make life evil on the whole. Pain and suffering may become relatively good on account of the moral discipline which they involve. But, if we are to look upon life as an education, must not that education be pushed further than we see it pushed here for the vast majority? The spiritual results of life to the vast majority seem, taken by themselves, to be as inadequate as its results in the way of pleasure or enjoyment. I cannot see how human life can be good on the whole when it is not good for the individual souls who live it. If we admit that life is unsatisfying and unintelligible from the point of view of most individuals, and yet seek to represent the whole course of nature as a beautiful picture of rational order and rational evolution, are we not really justifying the world's history as a sort of dramatic entertainment got up for the benefit of the superior people who are able to discover the secret of it all, who know the plot and can appreciate the "tragic irony" of the situations and the beautiful interconnexion—say, of Hellenic slavery and Hellenic culture? If life is only good upon the whole, it must be good only for those who see the whole. And after all, how many of us can pretend to derive much satisfaction from the survey of pain and sorrow, sin and imperfection, unjust destiny and unfulfilled aspiration which history discloses to him who looks upon it not as a many-hued kaleidoscopic show of impersonal laws and movements, actions and reactions, theses and antitheses and conciliations, but as the record of joy or sorrow, aspiration or despair, spiritual success or spiritual failure for individual souls?

Or if (as really seems to be hinted in some quarters)* all this tragi-comedy of human life is to be justified by the pleasure or satisfaction which it gives to a God who is personal enough to be amused but not personal enough to love, then such a God must be a Being who cannot with impunity be worshipped by men who want to become humane and good. Nor again does the history of the world justify itself to the moral Reason merely because some philosopher, or the deity whom he fashions after his own image, finds in it a beautiful and interesting illustration of his doctrine of categories.

But I must not stray further afield into the paths of speculation. I only just want to leave with you this thought—that belief in God and belief in Immortality must in the long run stand or fall together;

* See above, p. 14.

and that therefore, if we are not ashamed of faith in God, we ought resolutely to resist the habit of thinking or speaking in a hazy or apologetic manner about the Christian hope of Immortality, or seek a delusive refuge from speculative difficulties by nebulous talk about an Immortality which is not personal, as though we could attach any meaning to the idea of impersonal spirit. Faith languishes and dies unless, in worship and in other ways, we sometimes give it articulate expression.

The only people who (as it seems to me) ought to find a difficulty in believing in Immortality are those (and I believe they are few) who find it possible to think that Reason has got nothing to do with the world's making or sustaining, that history is a mere meaningless dance of independent and yet law-bound atoms which has as one of its incidental, accidental, purposeless effects or concomitants—consciousness, knowledge, virtue, sin, beauty, aspiration, conscience. That there are reasonable people who do not draw this great corollary from their faith in God, who do believe in a living God or at least in some inner reasonableness of things, who do recognise that conscience is more than a contraction of the diaphragm which somehow helps in the struggle for existence, and the human spirit more than a concourse of material atoms, which have inexplicably become conscious of themselves—that there are such people who yet find it easy to justify the world which we see around us on the supposition that there is no future after death for the individual human spirit—this is a fact which I can only explain to myself by the misrepresentations, the degradations, the caricatures to which the doctrine of Immortality has sometimes been exposed. But after all, it may be that those who let the coarseness of popular religionism in some of its forms blind them to the nobler side of the Christian hope are as unreasonable as those who suffer themselves to be so blinded by the dirt and dust of election campaigns as to see nothing in politics but a struggle among knaves for the outwitting of fools.

One of these misrepresentations is of so obvious and gross a kind that I am almost ashamed of having to notice it in this place. And yet one does occasionally hear intelligent and otherwise not ill-informed persons talking as if Christianity had made the hope of heaven and the fear of hell. into the sole motives of human duty. It will hardly be pretended that this is the teaching of Christ Himself or of the New Testament. The love that is selfish is no love at all, and the morality of the New Testament is summed up in the word love. When the Master taught that it were better for a man that a millstone were hanged about his neck and that he were drowned in the depth of the sea than that he should cause another soul to sin, we cannot believe that He was thinking wholly or chiefly of the physical pains of Hell. When He said, "Blessed are the pure in heart," He cannot have meant that it was as a mere arbitrary reward or premium that to this virtue was annexed the vision of God ; nor could men whose hunger and thirst after righteousness was really a hungering and thirsting after a carnal paradise find their reward in just being filled with that same righteousness. Nor is this one of those distortions of the Master's teaching which can justly be laid to the door of Theologians as a class. Had they been inclined so far to forget their Christianity, there was too much of Plato in the education of the Fathers and too much of Aristotle in the minds of the greatest Schoolmen to let them do so. Universal selfishness, duty for the sake of reward, life here and hereafter for the sake of pleasure—these are the doctrines of Christian Theology only at one or two periods of its deepest degradation. And, thank God, whatever may be the sins of preachers at the present moment, anyone who ascribes such teaching to the Churches of to-day must have been singularly limited or singularly unfortunate in his church-going experiences.

On the other hand, there is, I think, no reason for the lofty scorn which one sometimes hears expressed for those who put forward the consequences of sin in another life as a very powerful motive for effort and for self-discipline. We do not put aside the consequences of actions in *this* life—their consequences even to ourselves—in estimating their moral quality. We ought no doubt to look upon a single act of drunkenness, for instance, even where it has practically no physical ill-effects, as intrinsically unworthy and degrading. But to those who do not feel this, or do not feel it as intensely as they ought, we do not hesitate to represent the probable growth of intemperate habits with all their consequences—even their physical consequences, and still more their debasing effects on mind and character—as additional reasons for moderation and self-restraint. The wrongness of drunkenness does after all depend *partly* upon these tendencies. In exactly the same way we ought to admit—nay, most emphatically to assert—that temperance and chastity, love of truth and love of our fellow-men, are good in themselves—good for the life that now is, entirely apart from all thought of the life that is to come. Assuredly a man is not in a right moral condition who would be prepared deliberately to abandon the struggle to be pure and temperate, truthful and hard-working and charitable, on account of any loss or weakening of his theological belief. Assuredly he that does not will to do Christ's will for its own sake can never really understand His doctrine. But all the same we need not hesitate to admit that goodness and sin can rarely be the same things to the man who believes that in a few years it will make no difference to himself or to any of those whom his conduct may affect, whether he has worked and fought and struggled hard and unremittingly or weakly and fitfully or (it may be) not at all. Goodness and sin can with difficulty be the same things to him as they are to the man who sees in his own life and in the lives of those around him a stage in the development of immortal souls.

In the hour of weakness and despondency, to the poor and the suffering and the unfortunate and the much tempted, it is not easy to underrate the value of the doctrine of Immortality as a source of personal support, encouragement, and consolation. But it may well be that to many men in the full vigour of youth and prosperity, to whom life presents itself still as a fairly long series of opportunities both of enjoyment and of useful activity, to men whose ideas of happiness are healthy and whose ambitions and aspirations are generous and unselfish—to them it may well be that this is not the chief value of the Easter faith. To them it is not so much for themselves as for others that the idea of Immortality is the one condition of hopefulness—that hopefulness without which few men have the strength to lead effective lives. A living moralist has said: " When a man passionately refuses to believe that the ' Wages of Virtue' can be dust, it is often less from any private reckoning about his own wages, than from a disinterested aversion to a universe so fundamentally irrational that 'Good for the individual' is *not* ultimately identified with Universal Good." And so " we are not surprised to find Socrates declaring with simple conviction that ' if the Rulers of the Universe do not prefer the just man to the unjust, it is better to die than live.' " *

Such are the noble words of one who is after all compelled by his professed philosophy of pleasure to look upon the future life mainly from the point of view of reward or posthumous compensation. I will supplement them with the words of one whose faith in Immortality was of a more unhesitatingly Christian cast. "Evidently," writes Arnold Toynbee, " the starting-point of religion and philosophy is the same. It is the faith that the end of

* Professor HENRY SIDGWICK, *The Methods of Ethics*, Ed. iii. p. 504.

life is righteousness, and that the world is so ordered that righteousness is possible through human will." "If an astronomer show that the earth within a limited time must be destroyed, and the race with it, where is our hope of the happiness and perfectibility of the race? We want an eternal end: and this cannot be found in the good of the human race." And again: "Man lifts his head for one moment above the waves, gives one wild glance around, and perishes. But that glance, was it for nothing?" And from this point of view he can even say: "We do believe it would be irrational to try to be good if the course of the world were not ordered for holiness and justice."*

I will conclude with one more quotation which sums up all that I have been trying to say: "The more we think of reason as the highest thing in the world" (writes the late Master of Balliol in 1881), "and of man as a rational being, the more disposed we shall be to think of human beings as immortal."† And, we may add, all the reasons that we derive from the consideration of human nature in general, reach their maximum intensity when we think of human nature as it is exhibited in Jesus Christ, the Son of God.

* *The Industrial Revolution*, p. 246.
† *Life*, by CAMPBELL and ABBOTT, vol. ii. pp. 244, 256, 240.

XII.

THE CHRISTIAN DOCTRINE OF PROPERTY

Assize Sermon, preached before the University of Oxford, at St. Mary's, November 19, 1893.

"Neither said any of them that ought of the things which he possessed was his own; but they had all things common."—ACTS iv. 32.

THE first impression of anybody who read these words apart from their context would be, I suppose, that in the first days of Christianity there was established in the Church of Jerusalem a literal community of goods. A closer study of these early chapters of the Acts in their entirety must, however, result in a very considerable modification of this opinion. It will be observed that it is only those who possessed accumulated property who are represented as bringing their wealth into the common stock. Only those who possessed houses or lands (we are told) sold them, and brought the prices of the things which were sold, and laid them at the Apostles' feet. And even in their case, the story of Ananias goes to show that this surrender was not essential to membership in the infant Church, though, no doubt, more or less expected of well-to-do persons.

THE DOCTRINE OF PROPERTY 191

There is, however, no trace of the ordinary wages or earnings of the less wealthy being brought into a common fund. Nor, if we turn to the system of distribution adopted, does it appear that the whole community participated—still less that they participated equally—in the common property, except in so far as the 'Αγαπαὶ or love-feasts may have been held with sufficient frequency to constitute a partial approach to the ideal of a common life. In that daily distribution of money or food, at which Hellenist widows were neglected, there is no reason to believe that anyone participated except those who, like the widows—a class whose position in ancient society was a peculiarly hard one—were without the means of earning their own livelihood. And there are sufficient indications of the mode of life adopted by those early Christians of Jerusalem to make it quite clear that the system of charitable relief adopted among them fell very far short either of a communistic equality or of a monastic renunciation of individual property. Mary, the mother of John Mark, it is clear, lived in a house of her own, sufficiently ample to accommodate a large prayer-meeting, and she could afford to keep a maidservant.

What appears to have actually occurred was simply this: that the richer members of the community made large sacrifices to supply the needs of the poorer. "He that gathered much had nothing over, and he that gathered little had no lack." In short, the system of charitable relief adopted by the Church of Jerusalem differed rather in degree than in kind from the system of organized benevolence which played so large a part in the activity of all Christian Churches during the earliest and purest ages of their existence. The impression which this spectacle of active love made upon the world has long been one of the commonplaces of Christian apologetics. But it is only recently that we have begun to appreciate the extent to which the collection and distribution of common funds entered into the *raison d'être* of the Christian society, moulded its organization, and constituted the functions of its ministers. The beauty of early Christian life has never, perhaps, been more touchingly brought home to the modern mind than in Count Tolstoi's powerful story, *Work while it is called to-day*. But in one respect that great artist has done scant justice to the lesson which the life of the primitive Church has still to teach us. It was not merely (as he appears to suggest) by the wide diffusion of an enthusiastic spirit of brotherhood, not merely by a sort of extension to a wider society of the instinctive communism of the home, that the Christian Church did so much to expel from its midst alike the material and the moral evils of extreme inequalities in wealth. Without this enthusiasm of self-sacrifice mere machinery would, of course, have availed nought : but still we must not forget that it was by deliberate organization, and vigorous discipline, and statesmanlike administration that the Christian Church succeeded to so large an extent in exorcising the twin-demons of squalid poverty and selfish luxury. The first church-officials (after the Apostles themselves) whom the Church acquired were those Seven who have been quite uncritically described as the first Deacons, but who are quite as likely to have been the first Presbyters; and the Seven were appointed exclusively for the discharge of financial and eleemosynary duties, while in the pastoral Epistles among the qualifications demanded, not only of the Deacons but of the Presbyter-bishops, those of the ruler and administrator are at least as conspicuous as those of the teacher and preacher. So prominent was this social aspect of the early Church's activity that an outside observer might have been forgiven had he mistaken the whole organization for a great, world-wide Mutual Assurance Society, and its ministers for nothing more than the officials of a benefit club. The lamented Oxford scholar,* to whom we are so much indebted for recalling to our minds this side of the Church's early life, is sometimes indeed accused (not, I think, quite justly) of actually making this very mistake. But while we recollect that from the first the supreme end of the Church's existence was a spiritual one, we must no less emphatically recognise that those who cry out against the Church's interference in social questions, who want to make of the Christian Presbyter a mere preacher of sermons or a mere performer of sacred rites, who protest against his busying himself with questions of charity organization or social justice, of sanitary improvement or the amusements of the people, are really putting forward a theory of the Church's functions which is belied by the whole course of her history from the days of the

* Dr. HATCH, in his Bampton Lectures, *The Organization of the Early Christian Churches* (1882).

O

daily distribution at Jerusalem to the days of Mansion House Committees and Bishop Auckland Conferences.

If anyone doubts whether the words of our text, "they had all things common," is susceptible of the interpretation which I have given it, I should like to call his attention to the fact that, when Justin Martyr wrote his first Apology, he uses almost the very same expression as still applicable to the mode of life adopted by Christians in his own day. Whatever may be the case with the Jerusalem Church of the first century, it is quite certain that nothing like an actual renunciation of personal property obtained in the Church of Samaria in the middle of the second. There was no actual equality, no community of goods, no monastic or economic communism. But equally there was no selfish and ostentatious luxury on the one hand; no abject misery or unrelieved want on the other. "We," he says, "who once loved the getting of money and possessions more than aught else, now bring even what we have already into the common stock (εἰς κοινὸν φέροντες), and share it with every one in his need."*

We see, then, that in the days of Justin Martyr, no less than in the apostolic age, it was still true, in a sense, that Christians had all things common. Could that be said in any sense whatever of Christians now? And if not, why not? That is a serious question for us to face, and it is a question, I think, that, as Christians, we are imperatively called upon to answer.

Let us glance for a moment at the philosophical

* *Apol.* i. 14.

theories as to the basis of property. It was natural enough that Locke,* absorbed with the burning practical question how to secure person and property against the absolutism of Stuart kings, should have sought to invest property with a sacredness which would place it beyond the control of even the most lawful and beneficent of governments. The required speculative basis for the received Whig doctrine that a man could not be taxed without his consent was found in the theory that by the Law of Nature—by a self-evident principle which was prior to and independent of the social contract in which governments were supposed to originate—whatever a man mixed his labour with, that was indefeasibly his own. The doctrine was one which practically denied all rights whatever to the landless man, who could only live in a country by sufferance of its landlords. However little labour the supposed first occupier of land might choose to mingle with however much territory, not all the kings or all the parliaments or all the assembled manhood of the country could lawfully take from him a single acre. If a combination of landlords chose to grow no food upon their land, the rest of the inhabitants must starve without protest. Were a combination of landlords to prefer the scenery of a wilderness to the profits of agriculture and commerce, they could lawfully (it would seem on Lockian principles) compel the rest of its inhabitants to quit the country. In so doing they would not infringe upon the natural freedom of mankind, for are not the evicted population free to walk into the sea? To

* *Treatise of Civil Government.*

develope the logical consequences of such a doctrine is surely refutation enough. Yet it must not be supposed that the doctrine is dead. It lives still in the writings of not a few political philosophers, especially in America.* And a remarkable illustration has recently been afforded of the lengths to which *a priori* views of property may yet be carried in the great paradise of democracy, when the advocates of the United States in the Behring Sea Arbitration solemnly contended that the labour of letting the seals breed upon their shores gave them an indefeasible right against all the world to pursue them and capture them upon the high seas. It is true that the chief stress was laid upon the highly speculative psychology which attributed to the vagrant animals an *animus revertendi*, but that contention would hardly have served the purpose for which it was intended without the initial assumption that any quantity of the natural wealth of the Universe may be for ever appropriated by whoever chooses to take the trouble of first annexing it.

There is a much more popular doctrine abroad as to the basis of property, which after all rests upon essentially the same precarious foundations. It is the doctrine which seeks to base property upon the supposed right of every man to the products of his labour. It is forgotten that, as a general rule, labour creates no wealth without being "mixed" (as Locke puts it) with more or less of the raw material of the earth. And it will produce less or more wealth

---

* See, for instance, Mr. HERBERT SPENCER'S *Justice* and WOOLSEY'S *Political Science*.

according to the opportunities which each individual enjoys of access to the richest soil, the most precious minerals, or the most convenient harbours. Hence there is no possibility of estimating what the labour of each individual has produced unless we have already arrived at some laws for the previous distribution of the earth and its products. And then again, if we suppose this difficulty surmounted, even in the rudest society agricultural work requires some combination. Even in the rudest society the individual workman's labour would produce nothing unless he were secured by the assistance of the chief or the soldier or the organized village community against the hostile attacks of man and beast. And in our complex industrial organization it becomes every day more and more impossible to say how much wealth has actually been produced by each individual citizen. In the manufactory itself each piece of work is the joint product of many hands and many brains : and outside the manufactory its output could never become available for use or for foreign exchange without the co-operation of all kinds of social and industrial agencies. It is becoming more and more true every day that wealth is the product of the whole of society, exclusive of the idlers. That is true even of material wealth : it is still more true if we remember that a nation's real life consists not exclusively in the abundance of the things which it possesses. Hence, even if we admitted the abstract justice of the theory which seeks to find a basis for property in the inalienable right of every man to the labour of his hands and of his brain, the theory is one which turns out to be wholly incapable of practical application.

A priori theories of property are sometimes urged in a revolutionary, sometimes in a conservative interest. In the latter case they labour under an additional difficulty. Granted that it is a law of nature that a man should have an exclusive right to all that he can annex or all that the existing order of society enables him to accumulate, it will hardly be seriously alleged that it is equally a law of nature that he should be able to transmit it to whom he pleases. History teaches us how late a product of civilization this unrestricted liberty of bequest, which seems so natural to Englishmen and Americans, really is: while on the continent of Europe no such liberty actually exists. And if (with some violence to history) the provisions of continental codes are set aside as so many violations of natural right due to the wickedness of the French Revolution, we may remind ourselves of the provisions of the old Common Law of England, by which, from the growth of Feudalism till the time of Henry VIII., lands (with certain exceptions) could not be devised by will at all, while till a still more recent date a testator who left wife and children was unable to deprive them of two-thirds of his personalty. And if we turn to the distribution of the intestate's estates, it can hardly be a law of nature that in Sussex land should descend to the eldest son, in one part of the county of Kent to the youngest, and in certain other parts of the county of Kent to all the children equally. The only theory of property (as it seems to me) which will really bear examination is that which finds its justification in the social effects of the institution. It can only be justified, in so far as it is justified, in the same way in which anything whatever can be justified—be it a law or an institution or an individual human action:—by the end which it subserves. It can be justified only in so far as it tends ultimately to bring about the largest amount of *Good* on the whole (whatever we mean by "good") for society at large.

Property then is the creation of positive law. Historically it originated in custom, which was the earliest form of Law; and at the present moment no one of us could prove his title to what he calls *his* without citing the Common or Statute Law under which it has descended or been bequeathed to him, or to those from whom (in exchange for whatever services) he has received it. Property, though based no doubt on certain very deeply-seated instincts and tendencies of human nature, is still the creation of law; and what law has created law may alter, has altered, is altering, and will alter. The very same considerations of social expediency which justify the right of private property as the best means hitherto devised for stimulating the individual's energies in productive work must dictate its limits. To the framers of those American constitutions which declared the sacredness of property to be part of the law of nature, it seemed axiomatic that property in slaves was as sacred an institution as property in land, or that property in the services of others which is the real meaning of all other capital. Yet slavery has been abolished by Acts of Parliament and Acts of Congress. Every tax that is voted, every Act which imposes, in the interest of human life and health, fresh duties upon the owners of mines or factories or dwelling-houses, is as emphatic an assertion of the State's supremacy over property as the most high-handed confiscations of a revolutionary government. To what extent it is or may become expedient that this modification of private rights should ultimately be carried is a question about which reasonable men may hold very different opinions: and it is a question which I do not propose to discuss now. I merely wish to discuss the question of right. In questions of abstract right, theories which are not thoroughgoing are worse than useless: in questions of social expediency the shortest views are perhaps the best. And here perhaps it may not be wholly out of place to remark on the reckless short-sightedness of those who, believing (with all sensible Socialists) that it is only by the slow and orderly methods of legislative improvement that social progress can be achieved, still seem to lose no opportunity of encouraging every effort to bring contempt upon the law and its administrators, and to appeal on every occasion to mob violence as the readiest means of achieving their purpose. Those who believe most in the power of the State to bring about justice and better social conditions ought surely to be foremost in promoting a religious obedience to its laws, and an absolutely unflinching severity in their execution. Every addition that is made to the functions of the State is an addition to the duties of the Judge and the Magistrate, and only enhances the importance of maintaining the authority, the dignity, and the independence as much of the humblest rural bench as of the highest judicial tribunal. Those who doubt the wisdom of an unlimited increase of State activity do so (if they are wise) not so much on some *a priori* theory about the rights of the individual, as because they doubt whether a socialistic democracy would always possess the intelligence to place power and leadership in the hands of those who know, or exhibit the ruthless severity which would be needed in a society wherein idleness should be restrained only or chiefly by the terrors of the criminal law.

And now let us go back to the distinctively Christian aspect of our subject. If Christ be (as the Church has ever taught and as we believe) the supreme manifestation of that Reason or Wisdom of God which speaks also in the intellect and conscience of every human being, we might expect to find that His teaching would be in harmony with that of natural Reason. There are, indeed, those who think they can dispose (for Christian consciences at all events) of the uncomfortable demands of social reformers by simply referring them to the Eighth Commandment. Such persons might perhaps be puzzled to supply us with an intelligible definition of stealing other than "the taking of that which the Law declares to be another man's." But it is better perhaps to meet such objections by the broad principle that it was only by transcending it that our Lord professed to fulfil the

Mosaic Law. The eighth commandment *as such* is no more binding upon Christian men than the fourth. It is only in so far as it is deducible from the great law of love to God and man that it binds the Church of Christ to-day. There is therefore nothing in the Christian Law to confer upon property any greater sacredness than it can claim as a condition of social well-being. "Jure naturæ sunt omnia communia omnibus: per jura regum possidentur possessiones." "By the law of nature all things are common to all: it is through the laws of kings that possessions are possessed." That is the doctrine of the Canon Law about property, and it is based upon the teaching of St. Augustine.*

We may not, indeed, identify the eternal principle of Christian morality with the precepts of modern Utilitarianism or modern Philanthropism, without a word of protest. To love one's neighbour in the Christian sense is to love what is best and highest in him, to promote the best and noblest life for him so far as it is consistent with the equal claims of every other neighbour to a share in the best and noblest that life affords. And the Christian conception of this best and noblest is indeed a very different one from what logically ought (as it seems to me) to be the ideal of consistent Hedonism, and from the ideals which are sometimes actually presented to us in the writings of the baser sort of secularistic socialists. Christian love will not always promote maximum pleasure; Christian love, as has been finely said by

---

* AUGUSTINE, *Tract* vi. ad c. i. 25 Johannis: *Decretum Gratiani*, Pt. I. Dist. viii.

the most Christian of modern moralists, is the love of the ideal man in each man.* But while we affirm decidedly that the best social polity is not always that which promises the quickest abundance of food and raiment, the maximum of amusement and the minimum of work for the largest number of human beings, let us beware of that easy Optimism which tacitly identifies vague phrases about social stability or social order or social progress with the welfare and the predominance of that numerically insignificant class to which most of us in this Church belong. If the general diffusion of a low standard of material comfort is not always in the long run the best thing for the poor, the maintenance of our very much higher standard of material comfort and luxury may not always be really the best thing for us.

It is quite as much in the interest of the rich as of the poor that we desire to see a less unequal distribution of the national wealth. We are told by Aristotle in the best of all arguments against Socialism that it destroys the possibility of two of the greatest virtues—liberality and self-control.† It would be interesting to enquire how many of the virtues are made, to say the least of it, difficult for the possessors of great wealth, so long as they continue to live as the possessors of great wealth are expected to live. I do not at all seek to disparage the generous qualities that seem often to be positively fostered by wealth when it comes attended by hereditary responsibilities and traditions of public

* *Ecce homo*, chap. xviii.
† *Pol.* ii. c. 5 (p. 1263*b*).

service. But can it seriously be contended that the education of a rich man's son in England at this day is the best calculated to foster such virtues as humility, thrift, industry, temperance in its widest and highest sense, reverence for authority, respect and consideration for all sorts and conditions of men —in a word, a due sense of the relative importance of himself and other people? This is a question to which those who are so solicitous lest the morals of the poor should be corrupted by overmuch material prosperity might well be invited to address themselves. And, lest we fall into the pharisaic self-satisfaction which attends the condemnation of modes of life which are not within our own power, we may remind ourselves that many of us who enjoy what the world calls quite small incomes may yet find themselves practically in very much the same position—able to take our fill of all the pleasures and enjoyments for which we have really any mind, without feeling the faintest breath of social reprehension even from that portion of society which professes to make Christ's standard its own.

And this brings me to the point on which I chiefly want to insist. What may or may not be done by the State to bring about a less unequal, a juster, a more socially expedient distribution of wealth, this is not the time or place to enquire; even if it were wise to go, in such a forecast, very far beyond the next step which is warranted by the actual results of past experience. But what I want specially to suggest for our consideration this morning is this—that the same principle which justifies the existence of property should govern the expenditure of it by each member of a Christian society. The existence of property is justified only in so far as it tends to the common good: the expenditure of property ought to be governed by the same rule. There are undoubtedly many reasons (so far as I see, it will always be so more or less) which make it socially expedient and therefore right for the State to allow the individual to accumulate and to bequeath a much larger share of the wealth produced by the common toil than he could claim on any principle of abstract justice as the reward of his own personal exertions. But these political considerations do not require the individual to spend upon himself and his family all that the Law declares to be his. And as Christians we are bound to regulate our expenditure by the law of General Well-Being which (as I have tried to show) is, properly interpreted, identical with the Christian law of Love. By that it is not meant that the individual is to disregard altogether his own happiness even in the most material sense of the word. My happiness is of exactly the same intrinsic importance as that of anybody else. No man is required to love his neighbour better than himself. I could not, indeed, say with a philosophic Judge, that we are so constituted that the greater part—immeasurably the greater part—of my conduct ought to be regulated by a regard to myself and my own interests rather than by a regard to my neighbour and his interests. Even were the social effects of a general selfishness just tinged by Altruism so unexceptionable as this dictum seems to suggest, to admit such a rule of conduct without limitation or explanation would be to ignore the great Aristotelian doctrine that the unselfish man after all cares for the best part of himself. Still, the principle is sound in some things and to some extent. It *is* best in the general interest that we should each of us make reasonable provision for his own health, comfort, and happiness—in spite of the philosophical prejudice against pleasure, I am not ashamed to say his own pleasure—provided we remember always that the external goods with which we seek to provide ourselves can never be more than the conditions of any happiness which the Christian can call his good. Under existing circumstances (and probably under any circumstances that we need look forward to) the application of this principle will undoubtedly demand very considerable inequality in the distribution of the good things of life—even in that distribution which each of us has to make for himself of the material goods over which he has legal control. It would not be for the general good that we should all of us—there are of course exceptional sacrifices which may always be made by those whom God has called to them—but it would not be for the general good that we should all of us under all circumstances allow ourselves only such enjoyments and indulgences as might fall to our lot under some ideal distribution of goods. As things are now, a higher standard of comfort is demanded for the reasonable satisfaction of natural desires, and even for the due performance of social duty, in some classes than in others. And other things which hardly admit of rational justification in themselves are made necessary by social conventions and arrangements which cannot rapidly be changed. But, while making all allowance for these and many other practical considerations on which I have no time to dwell, I would venture to insist that neither any rational nor any Christian morality can justify any expenditure except in so far as it is in the long run, given the existing circumstances, on the whole best for the general well-being (including therein the individual's own well-being) that the wealth should be so expended.

And, after making all allowance for the necessity of more or less conformity with more or less irrational conventions, can it be said that the mode of living which is usual even among public-spirited and religiously-minded rich people really commends itself to the enlightened conscience as socially expedient? Or that the rich would not be better and as happy with fewer houses, servants, yachts, and horses? And are we not all of us tempted with every increase of income simply to mount one step higher on the ladder of luxury, or to make provision for doing so, or enabling our heirs to do so, at some future time? Are we not all apt to forget the perfectly indisputable truth that there is only a limited amount of wealth at any given time for the community to divide, and that it is not possible, by any contrivance or hocus-pocus of economic sophistry, to show that I can take more of it for myself without somebody else taking less?

It is not every one who has earned the right to offer much in the way of practical counsel or suggestion upon this matter of personal expenditure. Certainly I have none. And therefore I shall confine myself to laying down a principle, and leaving others to apply it to their own individual circumstances. But, to prevent misunderstanding, I will venture to add just two remarks, at the risk of seeming to some to be making excuses for capitalistic self-indulgence, and to others to be plunging into an abyss of socialistic extravagance. (1) I do not myself believe that for people situated as are most of us any very conspicuous or eccentric departure from the conventionalities of the society in which we live is at present what is really wanted. It is in that considerable margin of expenditure which social customs do leave within our own discretion that room should be found for the restitution to society of some part of whatever superfluous unearned wealth existing social arrangements may have made legally ours. And, if we steadily make this our aim, it may be that we shall be able in time to contribute just a little to make unusual kinds of expenditure which are now usual though not strictly necessary, and to make less necessary some things which may now be more or less plausibly considered necessary. (2) On the other hand, we must not for one moment lay to our souls the flattering unction that we can do our duty in this matter without some self-denial, and perhaps at times in some cases a little moral courage. We are not called upon to make ourselves miserable, or solitary, or ridiculous, or to injure our health or capacity for work, even though some of our wants may possibly be wants which would never be felt in a more healthily organized society. That would not be sociably expedient. It would clearly not be for the general good that no one should begin to enjoy his life till all wrongs were righted, all inequalities removed, and all misery abated. But still some things that we should like we must try to learn how to do without. Neither by any legislative improvement, nor by any ingenious device of economical philanthropy, will it ever be possible to make the poor about us a little more comfortable (as we all profess we should like to make them) without the rich becoming a good deal less rich (whether on compulsion or by their own voluntary abstinence), and without many of us who would never call ourselves rich being made or making ourselves a little poorer. The great work which lies before the Church of our day is to revive among Christians, not what I believe to be the completely imaginary and unhistorical communism sometimes attributed to the infant Church of Jerusalem, but some approach to that relative community of goods which enabled the early apologists all through the first age of the Church to boast that Christians still in a real sense had all things common.

XIII.

DIFFERENCES OF VOCATION

Preached before the University of Oxford, at St. Mary's, March 7, 1891.

"For the body is not one member but many."
1 COR. xii. 14.

IT is often assumed that religious differences relate wholly to Theology, while Morality is a matter about which all decent and well-meaning people are substantially agreed. I believe it would be truer to say that all the deepest religious differences which divide men and nations into hostile camps are ultimately traceable to differences of moral ideal. This is true of the profoundest religious divisions such as that which separates Christianity from Paganism or Mohammedanism: and it is true also of conflicting schools and sects and tendencies within the bosom of Christendom itself, especially of the great line of demarcation between Protestantism and Roman Catholicism. No doubt the moral ideal often survives for a time the Theology out of which it has sprung, while in other cases the Theology outlives the moral ideal which it created. The Christian ideal of life commands the homage of thousands among sceptical Europeans or educated Hindoos who reject the Christian Creed. On the other hand, if we go behind words and formulæ and get at things, the moral ideal of an enlightened modern Dominican like Lacordaire is as different as can well be conceived from the moral ideal which animated the Dominican Inquisitor of the Middle Ages. We may, indeed, thankfully acknowledge that as regards the fundamentals of the Christian ideal, stripped of foreign accretions and impurities, there is an agreement which often transcends the formal limits of the Christian Churches. But we should deceive ourselves, if we imagined that were Christian Theology to disappear as an effective force in moulding the minds of men, Christian Morality, at least, would still remain beyond the reach of criticism. If we have forgotten the intellectual history of the Renaissance, there is enough in the literature of our own age to remind us that a recrudescence of Paganism in belief is but too likely to bring with it a recrudescence of Paganism in morals. And if we penetrate behind a thin veil of conventional decorum (sometimes very thin), we shall find, I think, that the moral ideal actually taught by many writers (even in England) who cannot be charged with Paganism in any grosser sense, is nevertheless fundamentally opposed to the ideal with which Christianity is eternally bound up.

The symbol of the Christian Faith in all ages has been the cross, and the cross means nothing if it does not mean self-sacrifice. No one who accepts—I will not say the divine Nature or the divine Mission—but the moral leadership of Jesus Christ, can consistently accept any moral ideal which puts anything else above character or which estimates any quality of character more highly than Love. I do not say that the word "self-sacrifice" is by itself an adequate account of the moral ideal. I do not deny that the ideal of self-sacrifice has sometimes been taught by the Christian Church in a way which is at the least lamentably one-sided, even when it has not been pushed to the point of degrading superstition. When once self-sacrifice is inculcated as an end in itself, when once self-inflicted torture is regarded either as intrinsically meritorious and well-pleasing to God, or as at least conducive to holiness apart from the higher object for the sake of which the sacrifice is made, it is difficult to see on what grounds we can withhold our sympathy and our admiration from the Indian Fakir hanging suspended from a hook driven through his flesh, or extending an arm for a week together without rest or sleep. The moral ideal which found its highest expression in St. Simon Stylites, is, indeed, removed but one hair's-breadth from the moral ideal of the Fakir. But at the present time it can hardly be necessary to show that the Stylite ideal is not the ideal of Jesus or of his Apostles. By the best even among the ascetics of Christendom painful austerities are recommended only as the means to a higher life, even though some of them may differ widely from modern opinion and from St. Paul as to the profitableness of σωματικὴ γυμνασία for that purpose; and in the genuine teaching of our Lord Himself (when purged of the allusions to fasting introduced by later transcribers*), I think it will be found that self-sacrifice is always inculcated for the sake of others. Not the abnegation of self, but the preference for others over self is the essence of Christian morality.

When this explanation is given, it will be seen that there is no necessary antagonism between the moral ideal which takes self-sacrifice as its watchword, and the moral ideal which is expressed by those phrases so popular in the philosophical cant of our day—"self-development, self-realization, self-culture." Christian self-sacrifice only means the sacrifice of one part of the self to another and higher part. Self-development may be explained to mean only the development of the higher self—the social self—at the expense of the lower, the self-seeking, the individualistic self. We are all familiar with the hackneyed attempt to Christianise the self-love, the φιλαυτία, of Aristotle. But it will hardly be questioned that this effort to bridge over the gulf between the Christian and the Hellenic ideals really ignores fundamental differences. We have given up the attempt to harmonise Aristotle and Bishop Butler: and, if we turn from the ancients to the modern admirers of Hellenic morality, they would be the first to repudiate with scorn the gloss which the medieval commentators and the Oxford tutors of three generations back used to put upon the Aristotelian formulæ. It is of the essence of the ideal which the apostles of self-development propound that no part of the self shall be sacrificed. The

---

* In Mark ix. 29 the καὶ νηστείᾳ and in Matt. xvii. 21 the whole verse, are insertions rejected by Westcott and Hort and the Revisers.

animal elements in our nature are to have full play no less than the spiritual, the æsthetic no less than the moral, the self-regarding quite as much as the social, if indeed the intrusion of society and its claims is not resented as mere "parochialism" or mere fanaticism. At all events, it is the tendency of this Neo-Hellenic morality to put the intellectual above the altruistic impulses, to make individual culture a self-sufficing end, and to laugh to scorn all attempts to justify or to limit such culture by the requirements of social well-being, even when the widest and highest extension is given to the conception of social well-being. Development of the faculties, art for art's sake, poetry without preaching, novels without a purpose, description of life without criticism of life, self-culture without literary activity, passion without restraint, intensity at all costs, study without teaching—such are some of the notes of the school, or rather schools (for the tendency has various phases), which I have in mind. Indeed, the only way in which it is possible to find a definite content for the purely formal notion of self-development is to understand it as demanding the equal, or at all events the perfectly harmonious development of all the faculties and impulses of our nature. To assert merely that some development of all parts of our nature is desirable would be to assert what hardly anyone will deny. The most uncompromising of ascetics have condemned at least the more violent and rapid methods of self-destruction. The obscurantism of the Dark Ages allowed a certain development of the intellectual faculties—at least with a view to the comprehension of the constructions and syllogisms, the rhetorical tropes and figures, which they admitted to be contained in the pages of Holy Scripture itself. The question is how much development is to be accorded to the animal nature, how much to the intellectual, how much to the social? and in case of collision which is to give way to which? Hence the only intelligible meaning which can be given to this ideal of self-development is to understand it as implying an equal, all-round development in which no one part of man's nature shall be sacrificed to the claims of any other, still less the claims of individual perfection to those of social well-being. Now it may be worth while to consider for a moment not whether this ideal supplies a basis for either a Christian or a rational morality, but whether it supplies a possible, a self-consistent ideal of human life at all.

Take for instance the relation of bodily to intellectual development. The "mens sana in corpore sano" is of course a charming ideal. But there are different kinds of bodily health. And the health which is most favourable to intellectual activity is certainly not the rude health of the athlete or the fox-hunter. When a man who was once celebrated as an oar or a cricketer becomes a Bishop or a Judge, we commonly find the incident hailed by certain portions of the press as a welcome indication that athleticism is compatible with the highest intellectual achievement. And of course it is true enough that a few men do succeed in so far reconciling the conflicting claims as to attain high success in the schools, in athletics, and in after life. But this does not show that even these exceptional men have sacrificed nothing of their intellectual development to their athletic prowess. They have had time to row or play cricket, to read enough for a first class, and to get on in the world. But have they left themselves time to think? Moreover, the athletic success which such men obtain is seldom the very highest success—the success of avowed or virtual professionals: at all events it usually closes with their undergraduate career. Of course at this time of day it will be quite superfluous to insist that some active exercise is positively conducive to intellectual work, or that with some men a moderate athleticism is not inconsistent with very high intellectual development. All that I want to point out is the fact which will hardly be disputed—that as a rule the highest development of the bodily faculties is incompatible with the highest intellectual development. Body must be sacrificed to mind, or mind to body.

And so when we come to competing forms of intellectual activity, we shall find that it is impossible to develope one side of a man's intellectual nature except at the expense of some other. Specialism is (at least at the present day) the condition of doing anything considerable in any branch of knowledge whatever. A man may undoubtedly specialise in more than one direction, he may even make a speciality of the relations between two or more branches of knowledge—but specialise in some way he must. And specialism always means sacrifice. Just think for a moment of the sacrifices which a man must make to achieve any considerable piece of scientific or literary work. He must spend weeks, months, years over details which do very little for the general development of his own mental powers. He must be content to remain ignorant of things which other men know, not to read what everybody about him is reading, deliberately to narrow and restrict the range of his natural interests. It is not merely that his time is devoted to one particular subject, instead of being divided among several. The concentration upon one subject involves the exercise of certain faculties, the disuse and consequent degeneration of others. The reasoning faculties are developed at the expense of the imagination, or the imagination at the expense of the Reason. Philosophic subtlety is developed at the expense of literary power, or literary power at the expense of philosophic subtlety. Exactness is sacrificed to picturesque presentation, or picturesque presentation to exactness. The mind is stored with some particular class of facts or ideas, its capacity for some particular kind of observation is quickened and strengthened, while it contracts a proportionate incapacity for observing or dealing with other facts and ideas. Charles Darwin has told us how completely in his own case the contemplation of nature in her "subtilior metaschematismus" extinguished his once keen sensibility to her beauty and her poetry. We may fully admit the desirability of guarding (so far as possible) against the narrowing influence of highly specialised studies: we may assert emphatically that in most departments the man who is a mere specialist will not be a good specialist. But put as high as you like the importance of correcting the narrowness of specialism by general culture, and it will not avert the inevitable conclusion that high excellence in any department of intellectual effort is only attainable by sacrifice—by more or less sacrifice of one faculty to another, of one part of the self to another. The attempt at an equal, proportionate, all-round development can only end in sciolism, in mediocrity, in an ineffectual dilettantism.

And is it otherwise with the conflict between intellectual and practical or social claims? One would like to think there was none. But, if we look the matter in the face, one can hardly deny that what is best for a man's intellectual development is not always best for his moral development, if for the moment I may provisionally limit the idea of moral development to the development of the social activities and the social sympathies. For the sake of clearness let us take two careers, one practical and the other speculative, but in all other respects as like one another as possible. Let us suppose a man hesitating between the career of an East London clergyman, and the career of a student and teacher of Theology. Can there be much doubt that at the end of ten years of really earnest parish work in East London, sympathy for suffering, indifference to personal comfort and luxury, active zeal for righteousness and justice, personal devoutness, active hatred of evil, the conviction of the necessity of spiritual remedies for the disease of a sick world—can there be any reasonable doubt (I say) that in all human probability these qualities will be more developed, this side of the man's self will be more developed than would have been the case had the same man devoted those ten years mainly to the study of such matters as the origin of the Synoptic Gospels, or the evolution of Christian dogma? It is not fair indeed to state the case as if it were wholly a question of moral *versus* intellectual development: there is an antagonism between conflicting qualities even within the moral sphere itself. The speculative life has its virtues as well as the practical, though these virtues may rank lower in the moral scale. To say nothing of the laborious patience which is demanded by both lives, it is not only in knowledge, in intellectual insight, in subtlety, in acuteness, in breadth of view that the practical man will, sooner or later, fall behind the student. As a rule, the necessities of active work—especially of active religious work—are not favourable to love of truth (wherever truth cannot be made immediately available for purposes of edification or practical utility), to appreciation for opponents, to scrupulous accuracy of statement, to delicate discrimination between degrees of probability and so on. Here again it is clear that one part of the man's nature is necessarily developed at the expense of another. "There are very few," says Goethe, "who have a great mind, and at the same time are disposed to action. Intellect broadens our thought, but tends to weaken the will; action inspires, but it is liable to limit our breadth of view." One may fully and cordially admit that it is well for the practical man to keep up his studies, and for the speculative man to keep up his contact with practical life and practical human needs. Up to a certain point knowledge increases usefulness and experience deepens insight—but only up to a certain point. Here also it remains true that sooner or later one kind of development must be sacrificed to another. Excellence is only obtainable at the price of self-sacrifice. We have a choice of sacrifices, but that is all. Sacrifice there must be in every noble life. There is no such thing as abstract, all-round perfection. Whether it be a person or a thing, perfection is essentially relative. That is perfect which perfectly performs its functions. To seek for an ideal of the individual human life without regard to the needs of the complex society of which the individual is a member, without reference to the function which he is called upon to discharge in that society, is like asking what is the perfect form or the perfect structure of a particular feature or a particular member in the human body, apart from its relation to other parts with which it is in organic union. There may be a perfect lawyer or a perfect clergyman: there cannot, strictly speaking, be any such thing as a perfect man in the abstract. Indeed, if we push the matter further, the moral ideal cannot be quite the same for any two persons. No two persons are exactly alike either in the circumstances of their life or in their natural endowments: and the moral ideal for every man—in its actual content—is relative to these two things, circumstance and capacity. Every man's duty depends on his vocation: and the vocation of no two men is exactly alike.

The man is perfect, his true self is developed, when he is perfect after his kind, when he perfectly fulfils his true vocation; just as every leaf in the forest is perfect after its kind, though no two are exactly alike. The principle of self-development and the principle of self-sacrifice are harmonised by the principle of vocation. Apart from the principle that the development of the individual must be subordinated to the demands of the particular function which he is to discharge in a society, why should we withhold our respectful admiration from the exquisite intellectual cultivation incidental to a successful career in the higher branches of forgery? By all possible avenues of human activity self-development may be pursued; we can only say which direction, which kind of self-development is the true one when we look at the individual in his relations to the society of which he forms a part: and, when we do look at him in that light, it at once becomes apparent that the principle of self-development is only the reverse, the opposite side—as the convex to the concave—of the great Christian law of self-sacrifice. The anti-social self is sacrificed that the social self may be developed.

It may possibly be thought that what I have said as to the impossiblity of a perfect man in the abstract, is in some way inconsistent with the position which all Christians accord to Christ as the perfect man, the one true and perfect model for the imitation of us all. But Christ was not (if I may say so) a perfect man in general. He was a man who perfectly fulfilled a certain definite social function. The function which he discharged was indeed an absolutely unique one: his vocation was the highest of all vocations. All of us are called to follow him, but not all are called upon to follow him in the same way. All are called to tread in his footsteps, but not all are called upon to tread in them with equal closeness. The actual vocation which Christ discharged no other man can ever fulfil. His whole career was inspired by the conviction of His own unique vocation as the Messiah. He is the Head, we are the members. There can be but one Head of the human race. No other man's vocation can ever be the same as Christ's. Some vocations may approximate more closely to Christ's than others. In proportion to the measure of sacrifice which they demand, in proportion to the moral dignity of their service, is the approximation of other vocations to His. The vocation of the missionary approximates more closely to Christ's than that of the lawyer or the soldier. The work of rescuing souls from sin, the vocation of a Wesley or a Whitfield, of a Lowder or a Mackonochie, is (if we consider it in the abstract) morally higher than that of the student, the critic, or the historian, even though the subject-matter of his work be Theology, even though in the saintliness of his life he may tread in the footsteps of Green, of Lightfoot, or of Church. But vocations which in the form of their service may be less like Christ's are none the less necessary than the vocations which approximate most closely to His in their spirituality, in their austerity, in the weight of the cross which they impose. The task of the eye is nobler than that of the hand; but "the eye cannot say unto the hand, I have no need of thee," nor again the hand to the feet, "I have no need of you." Directly spiritual is higher than intellectual work: some kinds of intellectual work are higher than others; philanthropy is higher work than the ordinary business of lucrative trades or professions; and among professions some are higher than others: but all are necessary. One vocation differs from another vocation in glory, but all are necessary to the well-being of the body—Humanity—that body which, if it realized the ideal for which it was created, would be identical with the Body of which Christ is the Head. In one respect only all alike are called upon to a literal imitation of Christ. The work of all vocations requires self-sacrifice—different in measure, different in kind, but all alike are called upon to take up the cross and follow Christ by the surrender of their individual desires and inclinations to the perfect fulfilment of the task allotted to each in promoting the highest well-being of Humanity. In the perfect fulfilment of that task—never exactly the same for any two persons—lies the only true perfection, the only true self-development, of which each of us is capable.

When we compare the kind of life which most of us lead in a place like Oxford with the life involuntarily endured by the working classes of our own time, or with the life voluntarily adopted by the best parochial clergymen, it must be confessed that one is apt to be struck by the feeling that there is an unreality in attempting to bring the idea of self-sacrifice into connection with such a life as ours. Let me endeavour therefore to give a practical turn to the principle which I have been laying down, by two reflections.

(1) I have said that the true self which each of us is called upon to develope to the utmost extent of his capacity is the self which is most perfectly adapted for the service of his fellow-men in the particular relation of life wherein he stands. The self therefore which we are called upon to deny or to renounce is the self which is unadapted to that particular social function. All that stands in the way of our work, the work of our vocation, that is the first thing that we have to give up, that we are called upon to deny ourselves remorselessly. Perfect self-surrender to the work of our calling, the performance of every demand that it makes upon us as a religious duty, as a piece of service to our fellow-men—that is the primary, that is the most important kind of self-sacrifice which we are called upon to practise. It ought not to distress us, if we are sure that we have discerned our vocation rightly, that our service is less onerous and therefore in a sense less exalted service than that of some, that its demands are less exacting, that our work is found to be pleasant and accordant with our natural tastes and inclinations. Every vocation imposes some unpleasant duties: let us be content with performing them. Every vocation offers some opportunities of usefulness—even of spiritual usefulness. Let us make the most of them. The self that likes its work is the self to be developed freely, not to be denied.

(2) But besides the work of his calling or profession, everybody has clearly another life in which he may, he must if he is to be a Christian, practise some self-denial. The vocation of most of us in Oxford, whether we are here for a longer or a shorter time, the vocation of many of the ordinary secular professions to which Oxford men go when they leave Oxford, is a more or less easy and attractive one. The work of such vocations, however laborious, is generally more or less interesting. Compared with the work of the miner or the factory hand, even the drudgery of commonplace professions ceases to be very burdensome. And the life of such professions not only admits, but even demands, a good deal of what a Christian Apostle or a working man of the present day would call luxury. To confine ourselves to our own life here, there is a good deal of this luxury which we could not give up if we were willing to make the sacrifice, without more or less making ourselves less fitted for the work that we have to do here. It would not, indeed, hinder, perhaps it would aid our work as teachers and as students, if we did literally obey the Gospel precept by taking a little less thought than we do about what we eat and drink. But the individual would in most cases not do his work better, but worse, if he were to withdraw himself altogether from the social life, from the ordinary hospitalities, from the ordinary amusements of the place. The teacher and the student would become less fit for their work: the undergraduate would lose some of his preparation for future work. We should,

most of us, do our work, not better but worse, were we housed like working men, were we never to allow ourselves a holiday abroad, were we never to buy a book which we could possibly do without. A certain measure of comfort and luxury—in some cases a very considerable measure—is practically (for ordinary men) involved in the position in life to which we are called. But if that is so, surely we are specially bound to practice such self-denial as is possible,—such self-denial as will not destroy health, spirits, energy, contentment of mind, capacity for work. In order that we may fulfil our vocation as students, it is necessary that we should often turn a deaf ear to the cry of human misery,—that we should spend the bulk of our time on matters which may often seem trifling enough when we look to their immediate results, and then turn to the world with its sorrows and its sins, which we are doing so little directly to combat. It is right and necessary that we should do so; nobody will doubt *that*, who studies in history the disastrous results of attempting to confine intellectual culture to the immediately useful or the immediately edifying—the disastrous results of attempting to condemn intellectual life in the interest of Morality or Religion. It is right and necessary; but do we do all that we can to compensate for our lack of personal service by freely giving back to others some portion of the large share which we absorb of the wealth which the labour of others has created for us?

Such and such expenses and indulgences are

positively good and necessary, such and such others—in themselves hard to reconcile with the claims of our fellow-men—are practically inevitable under existing circumstances; but do we not sometimes unduly extend the bounds of the necessary and inevitable? Such and such concessions must be made to the requirements of hospitality, to social conventionalities, to our own acquired habits, to our own weakness, to the circumstances of our position; but do we not sometimes push such concessions to a point which practically means that we have adopted another ideal than that of the Cross?

Such are some of the questions which every recurring Lent, every approaching Holy Week, ought to bring before our minds—which we must answer for ourselves, each of us in the depths of his own conscience. For most of us, it is not what is ordinarily called asceticism, either in the stern sense which it bore when people really believed in the supreme excellence of self-torture, or in the attenuated form which it usually assumes in modern times, so much as simplicity, and moderation, and respect for the claims of others, which will form the best Lenten discipline in our time and station. Simplicity and moderation in pleasure and amusement of every kind, not only in Lent, hard work (not for six months of the year only), systematic liberality in giving—such (as it seems to me) is the true asceticism for our own day. All of them are necessary if we would (in any, however imperfect measure) realize the Christian ideal of self-sacrifice interpreted by the great Pauline principle of Vocation—the principle which calls upon us to develope the self most perfectly adapted to the work which our external position and our inward capacities point out for us, the work which the providence of God has assigned to each of us as members of the one body in union with Christ the Head.

XIV.

CHRIST AND CULTURE

Preached before the University of Oxford, at St. Mary's, 1897.

"And Jesus increased in wisdom and stature."—LUKE ii. 52.

SUCH are the words of the Evangelist. And here are the words of a commentator, no less a one than the great St. Bernard: "Semper Jesus virilem animum habuit, etsi semper in corpore vir non apparuit."* "Jesus had always the mind of a man, even though he did not always appear in bodily form a man." The Saint even goes on out of the fulness of his information to tell us that our Lord was a full-grown man even before his birth—"not less," he assures us, "in wisdom when conceived than when born, when small than when full-grown."

The history of the evasions, the sophistries, the dishonesties by which Theologians have attempted to explain away such statements as those of our text in the interests of a dogmatic theory about the Person of our Lord Jesus Christ is one of the most curious chapters in the history of human thought. The controversy as to the limits of Christ's human knowledge is a very old one. It occupies a prominent place

---

* Hom. super *Missus est*, ii. 10, quoted by Canon GORE, *Dissertations on subjects connected with the Incarnation*, p. 167 (note).

both in the later patristic age and in the age of the Schoolmen. And in both periods there were men of unblemished orthodoxy who declined to outrage common sense and to distort the language of Scripture by representing Christ as a non-natural man in whom the indwelling Logos had practically removed all the limitations necessarily involved in a true humanity. A very little thought is necessary to show that if Christ really knew everything, knew all the facts of Physical Science, of History, of Criticism; truths which it has taken many thousand years to accumulate, truths of which not one-twentieth part can be mastered by the most gifted individual in the longest lifetime, and which taken together must form but an infinitesimal part of the all that there is to know—if He knew all this, without having ever learned, He would not have been in any true sense a man. The medieval Realist might see in Him the union of an abstract humanity with an abstract divinity, but such a humanity could have had nothing in common with the humanity that we know, with the humanity that in each one of us cries out for someone to help it in its aspirations after the knowledge and the love of God. To ascribe such a knowledge to Christ is to destroy the very idea of an Incarnation. Not many years ago the notion that such doctrine was necessarily implied in the Church's doctrine of the Divinity of Jesus Christ was slowly eating away the faith of many who were crying out for a rational belief. It was possible for a popular novelist to represent a highly-educated clergyman as surrendering all faith in historical Christianity because he had come to the conclusion that the book of Daniel was not a true piece of history—a fact supposed to be included in the general guarantee which our Lord was represented to have given to the plenary inspiration and historic infallibility of the whole Old Testament. We cannot be too grateful to the living Theologian* whose courage and learning have made it possible without concealment and without reproach to adopt the view of the greatest Fathers and of the boldest Schoolmen as to the limitations of Christ's knowledge; and to take in literal earnest the doctrine of the New Testament and of the Church of England: "Christ in the truth of our nature was made like unto us in all things, sin only excepted."

But I do not wish to-day to dwell upon the dogmatic aspects of our text. I want rather to draw a practical lesson from this simple statement that Jesus Christ had to learn, that He spent (as is implied by the words of our text) some years in intellectual study, and that such study was necessary to fit Him for the unique task which lay before Him. We are so familiar with the idea of our intellectual debt to Greece, and our moral and religious obligations to Judea, culminating in the supreme debt that the world owes to our Lord Jesus Christ, that we are perhaps apt to overlook the intellectual side of His work. Nobody will deny the vast amount of truth that is contained in that striking generalisation of Sir Henry Maine's: "Everything in the world that moves is Greek in its origin." The more the ultimate sources of the Philosophy, the Science, the Mathe-

* Canon GORE.

matics, the Medicine of the Arabs and other Oriental peoples are explored, the more clear does it become that in such matters the function of the Semitic peoples was adaptation, transmission, development, rather than origination. But sometimes an *a priori* theory as to the Greek origin of the world's greatest ideas finds expression in baseless attempts to affiliate even religious ideas of Jewish and Christian origin to various phases of Greek philosophic thought: while the same prejudice also causes Christian minds to overlook the intellectual greatness of the Jewish prophets and the intellectual revolution which was effected by the appearance upon the stage of history of Him whom we reverence as the Son of God. True it is that in the main the work of Jesus was moral and spiritual, not intellectual. The truths that He came to reveal were intensely practical moral and religious truths, not truths of Philosophy, or Science, or Criticism. It is the character of God, His moral relation to us and our relation to Him, not the laws of His government in the Physical Universe, that we see reflected in the life and consciousness of Jesus Christ. The purpose too of His work was all primarily moral—to change men's hearts and wills, not to instruct their intellects. His method again was primarily moral, not intellectual. He appealed to the conscience rather than to the speculative intellect: He moved men by personal influence rather than by intellectual cross-examination. And lastly He founded a Church, whose terms of communion are primarily moral—attachment to a Person and to an

Ideal—not a school whose unity depends upon intellectual agreement.

And in this contrast of method lies no doubt the secret of His success (if we may reverently say so) as compared with the failure of the Philosophers. But for all this, we must not overlook the fact that the teaching of Jesus Christ did constitute an intellectual revolution; and that this intellectual revolution was a necessary part of His spiritual work. The destruction of paganism, with all the enormous intellectual advance which that implies, was His work, not that of the Philosophers. It was due to Him that the world accepted, freed from all Jewish narrowness, that magnificent conception of the world as a universal order—the effect of a single cause—which the Jewish prophets had slowly built up. Do we, again, often enough remember the earnestness which has been lent to the pursuit of truth by the breaking down of the gulf which in ancient thought divided speculative thought and religious practice, ethical theory and social organization? For that too was the work of Christ and His Church. A time was to come when ecclesiastical influences should in practice be unfavourable to the recognition of the supreme value of truth. But that was not till Religion had ceased to be purely religious and had become political. And after all, even the logomachies of the post-Constantinian Church were in their way a homage to truth. The ancient world knew little of persecution, just because as a rule nobody cared enough about truth to attempt putting it into practice. And truth begins to excite hatred and opposition only when you begin to live it out. Just because Christianity was the first great attempt—the first great ecumenical attempt at least—to mould the whole of life, personal and social, upon a reasoned theory, it brought with it not peace but a sword.

And all these intellectual results of Christ's life were not accomplished without intellectual work. No reverent mind which acknowledges in the consciousness of Christ a revelation of the Supreme, not to be placed merely on one line with those other revelations which have prepared the way for it or completed its development—no such mind will insist on building up a detailed or elaborate theory as to the relations between our Lord's human thinking and the Divine Wisdom or Logos which revealed itself in Him. But this at least the facts warrant us in saying. It was not without diligent study of the Hebrew scriptures, not without real *thinking* that Jesus did his unique work as Messiah, Redeemer, Son of God. To recognise—fully and unreservedly—the activity of the human brain in the production of those words which have proved the spirit and the life of the world no more diminishes from the divineness of the revelation which they enshrine than the recognition of the activity of a human will in the deeds which form no less real an exhibition of that mind and character in which God is eternally revealed.

And now let us dwell upon the practical significance of this fact. One of the difficulties which we encounter in attempting to make the life of Christ a model for our own imitation is the great difference between the actual occupations of His life and what many of us feel are, must be, ought to be, the occupations of ours. The public life of Jesus—the life with which most of the Gospel narratives are occupied—consisted for the most part in teaching of a directly practical, ethical, religious character, and in healing the sick. We recognise easily enough the opportunity of Christ-like life in the work of the Pastor, the Physician, the Hospital Nurse, the Missionary, the Philanthropist. And perhaps, enlightened by such teachers as Sir John Seeley or living writers whom I need not name, we may not even find it difficult to discern in the work of Charity organization, of Sanitary Committees, and other voluntary efforts at social reform, of Poor Law Guardians and School Boards and County Councils, when these are pursued in the spirit of self-denying human brotherhood, opportunities for lives quite as Christ-like as those spent in the spiritual teaching of individual souls or the personal ministration to individual bodies. It is more difficult to see how the intellectual life can be Christ-like. For us whose main business here—whatever subordinate tasks we rightly take up—is to be students, whether for a longer or shorter time, it may not be amiss to dwell awhile upon the fact that the life of Jesus Christ did include much intellectual activity. Christians may then freely recognise intellectual activity as an element in the Christian ideal of human nature, though we must proclaim also that even intellectual self-development must be made subordinate to that service of the brethren in which Christ taught us that the highest life of the individual consists. True intellectual life, like true practical life, must, in a sense, find itself by losing itself in the life of others.

Most emphatically must we assert against the defenders of an anti-social 'self-realization' that the student and the artist are bound as much as other men to recognise the claims upon them of their fellow-men. Intellectual goods must be consecrated, like other good things, by being shared with others—in one way or another—by teaching, by professional work, by public service or the like. The primitive idea of sacrifice, we may remind ourselves, is not self-annihilation, but communion. I am referring of course to the kind of intellectual work which becomes the business of life, not the mere adornment and refreshment of it. In due measure it is undoubtedly good and right to enjoy intellectual pleasures which have no social consequences. If a thing is good for me to give to my neighbour, it cannot be wrong for me in due measure to enjoy it myself. It could not for instance be lawful for me to devote my life to writing novels which it would be a sinful waste of time for another man to read. Intellectual culture is an essential part of that true well-being of humanity which Christ bid His followers to promote—more important than mere physical satisfaction, though inferior to its highest spiritual and moral needs. Intellectual work must be sanctified and christianised, as all other work is sanctified and christianised, by being in some way or other turned into a branch of social service.

It is a materialistic theory of life after all which

acknowledges the possibility of Christian service in the work which ministers to bodily wants and denies it in the work which supplies humanity even with such intellectual luxuries as various readings, or occasional verse, or antiquarian theories. But in the sphere of intellectual work, as in other spheres of life, we must recognise that not all services can claim the same moral dignity. Some vocations are higher than others. Not all men have the same vocation. The less important tasks in the service of mankind must be performed as well as the most important—the pleasanter tasks as well as the more arduous. All social service is Christian. But there are some kinds of intellectual work in which (if in some ways and to some men they demand less severity of sacrifice than more active life) it ought to be specially easy to recognise the possibility of Christ-like service. I do not know that we sufficiently appreciate the great service which the Mendicant Friars have rendered to the Church by their consecration of the student's life. When we think of a Friar and a Friar's work, we naturally think first of toilsome preaching-journeys and sick-bed ministries, of spiritual counsel and sympathy for sick and poor. But this was not the only side of the Friars' work. It was mainly to the Friars that Europe owes the absorption of Aristotle into the thought of Christendom. It was the Friars who appreciated, as men had never appreciated before, how a life of love might be spent in diffusing knowledge—secular knowledge no less than religious knowledge—of which humanity had sore need. There are no doubt departments of knowledge in which, however fully we may be persuaded of their ultimate social value, a too clearly conceived and conscious utilitarian aim would be injurious to the study. There is political guidance to be got out of the study of History, but the historian who conducted his researches primarily in quest of political morals would be a bad historian. There are practical discoveries to be got out of Physical Science, but it will often be most abundant where the "fruit" has not been sought. But there are other branches of knowledge in which (so long only as we resist the temptation to make truth give way to immediate edification) the direct consciousness of a practical aim is eminently beneficial to the best interests of the Science itself. And it is well, I think, that we should distinctly realize the imperativeness of the social demand for knowledge of certain kinds. Never in the history of the world has it been truer that the people perish for lack of knowledge. Never has it been more necessary that those who possess knowledge should become, if I may so say, missionaries of knowledge. There is indeed a social value in all knowledge. One of the best things we can do for other people, whether for individuals or for classes, is to help them to love and to enjoy the knowledge and the culture which we enjoy ourselves, even without direct reference to any more practical social end. But in two departments of life, especially and more directly, we are called upon — even the most ordinary of students, and the least intellectual of educated men are called upon—to listen to the cry of a people perishing for lack of knowledge.

(1) Firstly, in the whole region of political, social, and economic thought. Here there is eminently a sphere for the discoverer. Economic problems want solving which have the directest practical bearing upon the duties of the rich and the lives of the poor; and patient, self-forgetful, unassuming study of very small questions will all tend in due time to the solution of very big questions. And there is a still more urgent need for the diffusion of the knowledge that we possess. Here there is work to do for the humblest economic student and even for people who can hardly claim to be that. We still hear noble lords who pose as statesmen gravely justifying racing because it gives so much employment. Oxford is still the happiest hunting-ground of tramps and beggars because so many educated men do not know the harm they do in giving to them, or what they ought to do with the money that they waste in that and other ways. And, if we take a wider view of things, really it is no exaggeration to say that the issue of the great democratic social experiment upon which inevitably, as much under Conservative governments as under Liberal governments, we are now entering, depends mainly upon the extent to which it shall be found possible to diffuse among the people and their leaders sound ideas upon great social, political, and economic questions. If they believe the demagogue who tells them that the "social revolution" can be accomplished in five years, it will not be accomplished in

500. If they hearken rather to those who say that something like Socialism in this country might be possible if it were not for the Socialists,* I will not say that the dreams of the Socialists may be accomplished, but there may be in store for this country a future which shall as far exceed the glory of materialist Utopias as the glory of Christ's Kingdom has already exceeded the glory of the military Messiahship foretold by the prophets of Israel.

It was a dream, if you like, of Plato's when he supposed that the idea of the Good was to be reached chiefly by the study of Pure Mathematics, but it was soberest reality when he pronounced that the future well-being of humanity depended upon the possession of knowledge by a class who would regard it not merely as a priceless enjoyment for themselves but as an equipment for the highest tasks in the service of their fellow-men.

And there is another department of life in which the people perish for lack of knowledge—I mean in all that relates to the sphere of Religion. Here too there is room alike for the profoundest thinker, for the most patient of students, and for the humblest intelligent Christian who will really make the effort to add to his faith a little knowledge. On all sides men's religious ideas are being shaken, changed, transformed by the advances of historical and critical enquiry, and by the growth of new philosophical ideas and new ethical ideals. There is a demand for a great reconstruction of Christian Theology, such a reconstruction of Christian Theology in the light of

---

* The remark is due to Mr. Bernard Shaw.

our improved knowledge of the Universe as Thomas Aquinas accomplished for his own day at the great crisis when the recovered works of Aristotle represented the world's richest intellectual inheritance. The mere handful of men who are seriously engaged in that great task want many helpers, and still more they want missionaries of the knowledge which they are building up. When we turn from the cultivated few to the great mass—let us say even of ordinary fairly educated people, what a chaos there is in religious belief and no-belief! Everywhere we find religious belief losing its hold on the minds of men on account of the silence of the instructed clergy, the flimsiness of the religious ideas which are taught by the less instructed, and the vagueness and indefiniteness of the only substitutes which are offered in their place by those who have parted company, or all but parted company, with the Christian tradition.

And we go on perpetuating this chaos by the religious teaching which is provided at home and at school. We go on teaching children things which we do not believe ourselves. Or we do not teach them anything definite at all. We subtly insinuate into the minds of children and schoolboys our own disbeliefs, and we do not teach them why it is that the story of Jesus is more credible and more important to human souls than the biographies of the Patriarchs. It would be ungrateful not to acknowledge the enormous services which great Headmasters like Dr. Arnold and his many followers have rendered in the matter of religious education. Yet even in public schools the theological chaos of the master—sometimes based simply upon ignorance and want of study where it is not based upon indifference and neglect—too often reflects itself in the mere repetition of an unbelieved tradition, or in insinuations which simply destroy without rebuilding, or in a frank substitution of Syrian geography and Greek paradigms for the religious lesson which it is his duty to give. And if we turn to the ordinary Sunday School, it may be doubted whether there are twenty Sunday or elementary Church Schools in the kingdom where the altered ideas of the clergyman have introduced any appreciable change in the received manner of teaching the Old Testament. What wonder then if we are told that the secularistic lecturer is invariably the ex-pupil of a Sunday School? What wonder if the fanatics of secular education fail to see that the Scripture lesson, properly conducted, may be made the most interesting, the most intellectually stimulating, the most philosophical lesson of the whole week? I do not ignore or underrate the tremendous difficulty of this task which lies before us, the task of popularising the best Theology of our day; still, it has got to be faced, and everyone who will be a clergyman, a schoolmaster, or even a parent must do his or her part in facing it. But be it noticed that, difficult as some of the questions before us may be, there are some things so plain and so easy that every man who will take the trouble to acquire the most elementary information, everyone who will be bold enough to give open expression to ideas which are now scarcely matters of dispute with instructed Theologians of any school, may really contribute something towards this great end of freeing Christian belief from the unnecessary accretions with which so many uncritical centuries have laden it. Everyone who takes the trouble can understand the conception of a gradual or progressive revelation, that revelation is not confined to Judea, that revelation is not the same as historical infallibility, and so on. Yet if these simple ideas were widely taught, half the difficulty would be gone. For remember that here in enlightened Oxford there are still people who do not see how they can believe in Christianity at all if they do not believe that the sun stood still or that Balaam's ass spoke. And among thousands of the less instructed every idea about God and Christ, about Duty here and Immortality hereafter, is being swept away by the pot-house dialecticians who regard the question "Who was Cain's wife?" as a sufficient refutation of the claims of Christianity.

"Freely ye have received, freely give." That must be the maxim for every Christian student. In respect of intellectual wealth as of other wealth, we want to realize more fully than we do the responsibilities of possession. And there is one class of course upon whom there rests an especial measure of this responsibility. Is it sufficiently realized what exceptional opportunities the position of a parochial clergyman gives for the diffusion of knowledge—especially knowledge of these two kinds, the political and economic knowledge which is necessary for social salvation, and the intellectual religious knowledge which, though it is not the *unum neces-*

sarium, is in these days to so many the all but essential condition of their soul's health? On all sides of us the life of souls is withering because they do not know how to use or understand the Bible when they have given up mechanical and impossible theories of inspiration; how to pray without disbelieving in the laws of nature; how to believe in and worship and imitate Christ as the supreme Revealer of God to us, though some of the traditions about Him may seem to them more or less uncertain and some of the Church's formulæ about Him scarcely intelligible to men who are not theological experts. Arnold Toynbee used to say that two things were essential for the work of the priest — sympathy and knowledge. Sympathy— sympathy of the particular kind which is needed for such work—is a rarer and a diviner gift than knowledge: it does not always go with knowledge. Without some measure of it no doubt the work of the parish priest cannot be done. But it is no substitute for knowledge.

It is impossible for us who live here in comfort and enjoyment to reverence too highly the lives which are led by our brethren in the crowded alleys of large towns, where often the time and opportunity or sometimes even the desire and capacity for knowledge are all but wanting. But is there not a danger lest the very severity of the ideal which these men set before themselves may frighten away from the Church's Ministry men of whom she has much need, men who have intellectual needs and intellectual interests and intellectual enthusiasms? They would fain sacrifice much to employ them in the service of the Church if they were encouraged to believe that the Church wanted them: but they do not feel that they would be really serving God or man by committing a kind of intellectual suicide. Might not such men be more often won for the service of the Church if it were better understood that the clergyman is a teacher, and that if he is to teach to any purpose he must also be something of a student?

I am not for one moment urging that anyone should take holy orders who does not believe that Christianity contains for this age as for former ages a true revelation of God, and who does not feel a real desire to help other people to lead Christian lives. But the intellectual interpretation and presentation of Christian truth must needs keep pace with the changing needs and the expanding knowledge of successive ages. An unthinking acquiescence in every detail of traditional Theology is no qualification for the Church's Ministry, nor is a lively sense of some of the weaknesses of the ecclesiastical temper a disqualification. In every age in which Theology has been really alive, Theology has been a growing Science: where there is life, there is growth. And therefore the Church does want for her service men who will love the truth, who will diligently seek the truth, and will have the courage to proclaim whatever truth may be revealed to them. Such men are wanted even for the most practical work among the poor. The possession of superior knowledge, when the knowledge is placed at the command of love, is one of the most effective recommendations to the confidence of the best working men. The clergymen who most boldly speak their real mind on theological and social matters are the men whom they trust most. And after all the upper and middle classes have souls too. There are, to say the least, large numbers of them who want to be helped to think and to believe intelligently, and to act upon reasonable views of social duty and of Christian faith. And they will not be able to get that help unless thoughtful, studious men (not of course necessarily men of conspicuous or showy abilities) will sacrifice something to come and teach them—will sacrifice careers that are more attractive from the point of view of ambition, of profit, and of inclination for the sake of Christ and His Church. Men are not generally brought to Christ by argument or intellectual enlightenment, but they are very often most grievously kept back from Him by the want of intellectual light. Unless the teaching side of the priestly office be duly recognised, as well as its yet higher functions of sympathy and inspiration and practical service, the Church will never claim the undivided allegiance of her members. Their sympathies will be Christian, but not their intellects. And if the soul is not wholly Christian, the life will not be wholly Christian either. "Jesus increased in wisdom." The Church must increase in wisdom likewise, if it is to be in very deed the body of which He is head.

XV.

THE IDEA OF THE CHURCH

Preached before the University of Oxford, at St. Mary's,
1897.

"The church of the living God, the pillar and ground of the truth."
1 TIM. iii. 15.

THE theological controversies about the Church have centred round the question whether the true Church of Christ is visible or invisible. If the question be put broadly and nakedly, there cannot be much doubt or difficulty about our answer to it. If the Church means merely a number of individual persons predestined to everlasting salvation, living isolated, unrecognised, and unrecognisable by one another in the midst of a society whose organization takes no account of this unascertainable membership—such a conception of the Church destroys the very nature of a human society. A mere collection is not a society, even where it consists of known individuals. It destroys the essence, as Aristotle or St. Paul might say, of a κοινωνία; or if we like to express ourselves in the fashionable but somewhat misleading cant of the hour, we might say that a society must be an organism, and a number of human beings can hardly form an organism when their action and interaction, their common work and their common life, is of a kind which is inaccessible to human observation. An invisible Church is a contradiction in terms. Equally untenable is such a theory if we turn from the idea of the society to the end which it is to serve. Whatever else we may doubt about the Church, it will hardly be disputed that it is a society which has a mission here on earth to fight against that merely natural, unspiritual element in human society which is called in the New Testament "the world." Is there anything that the world would rejoice at more heartily—is there anything that would serve its purposes better than that the Church of Christ should be as unorganized, as inconspicuous, as invisible as possible? An invisible Church would be an impotent Church.

But if we reject the theory of an invisible Church, do we necessarily admit that the tremendous things that are said of the Church, whether by our Lord Himself or by the Apostles and early fathers, can really be applied to the actual, visible, tangible society which history speaks of as the Church, or to any or all of the bodies which it speaks of as Churches or as sects? Is it true that admission into this body by water is as necessary to inheritance of the Kingdom of Heaven as the Baptism by the Spirit? Can anyone seriously contend that any particular Church or all the Churches together have always taught the truth and never taught anything but the truth, or that all the bindings and loosings of every tumultuous Synod or worldly Bishop have been or will be ratified in heaven? Surely it is scarcely possible for any reflecting person to say 'Yes' to such questions, and yet that is what we must do if we are to identify the Church of Christ's promises and of early Christian theory with any actual, visible, organized human society.

Let us dwell on this difficulty with reference to two of the main ideas connected with the Church— its duty in the matter of doctrine, and its powers of discipline.

(1) First then its function as to doctrine. The Church, we are told, is "the pillar and ground of the truth." Certainly it is part of St. Paul's conception of the Church that it should be the depository, the teacher, the interpreter of spiritual truth. Certainly there are promises of Christ's continual presence and guidance made historically to His actual disciples, but which we can hardly be wrong in applying in some sense to the Church of all time. It is difficult, indeed, to see what conception of the Church would not include in itself the idea at least of teaching and preserving, if not of interpreting and developing, the faith which Christ committed to His disciples. Are we then to say that the historic Church has not erred? Surely such an assertion could only be made out by reducing the idea of a Church to a mere tautology. If we say that the Church is the body which teaches the truth, no doubt we may hold that the Church has not erred. But then that implies that we know from some other source what

is the truth, and renders nugatory the attempt to make the judgment of the Church the criterion of truth or error. Moreover, the whole conception of infallibility, if it is applied to the actual concrete determinations of synods and councils, implies a reliance upon mere majorities which seems utterly inconsistent with any spiritual or worthy view of the Holy Spirit's working. If we say that the Monophysites *must* have been wrong because they were outvoted, what becomes of the Western revolt against the Eastern majority or of our own resistance to the decrees of Trent?

(2) And then if we turn to that other great function of the Church, the power of binding and loosing, that is, the power of defining, fixing, interpreting, applying, the moral ideal, are we to say that the actual historic Church (define it what way you will)—are we to say that any particular, historical, visible society upon earth has never actually called good evil and evil good? Here surely (whatever may be the case with doctrine) we cannot limit the voice of the Church to the decision of ecumenical or of any other Councils, for conciliar decisions have not, until very modern times, dealt much with morality as distinct from doctrine. And if we look to the actual teaching of the living, working Church at any one time, can we say that the Church has ever held up to the world a perfectly pure representation, a perfectly legitimate development of the teaching of her Founder? Does not every reasonable historian of the Church—no matter what his theological position—admit more or less

emphatically that the Church of one age preached celibacy to the disparagement of Christian marriage, that the Church of another age or of the same exaggerated asceticism at the expense of ordinary morality, and monastic contemplation at the expense of patriotic and private duty; while those who would have most sympathy with these tendencies would agree neither with what would seem to them the worldly laxity of the Protestant Churches nor with the casuistical laxity of post-Reformation Romanism? Or if we turn from general moral principles to their particular application—from the binding or loosing of acts to the binding or loosing of persons—who will maintain either that all excommunications have been just, or that excommunications which are not just are ratified in heaven?

What are we to say then to these antinomies? The Church must be visible or it is no Church. And yet if it is visible, we cannot find in actual history or actual life the Church which corresponds to Christ's promises. Is it not clear that in all the New Testament teaching about the Church of Christ we are presented with an *ideal*—an ideal of what Christ's Society was meant to be; an ideal which she is meant to realize, which to some extent every community of Christians has realized, but which no Church of any one time or place—no, nor the whole Church of all times and places, has ever actually attained? Just in so far as the Church has answered to her ideal, so far can she claim that the tremendous things that are spoken of the ideal Church are true of her. Just in so far as she has fallen from her ideal, these things cease to be true of her; just so far the Church ceases to be the Church at all.*

Do you say that if we reduce this conception of the Church to an ideal, we deprive it of its value? Yes, certainly, if what you want is a mechanical and unspiritual test of spiritual truth and spiritual life, then the conception of the Church as an ideal does become useless. If what Christ says of the Church is wholly and absolutely true only of the ideal

* For a full examination of the New Testament doctrine as to the Church see Dr. Hort's *The Christian Ecclesia* (1897), the result of which seems in the main to support the view here taken. Among earlier writers who have maintained the ideality of the Church I may mention Myers, *Catholic Thoughts on the Church of Christ and the Church of England*, and Mr. Llewelyn Davies in many published writings. It is partially recognised by Prof. Stanton: "I would premise that there will be before us an ideal which is far from being anywhere fully, and which has never been more than approximately, realized. Yet there may be, and I believe are, broad distinctions in the extent to which different communities of Christians depart from it, such as will justify the view that some are portions of the Church and others are not." (*The Place of Authority in Religious Belief*, p. 195.) I could accept the last clause if it is meant to apply to the community in which Christian love is wholly extinct, not if it is meant to apply to communities which are irregular about orders and sacraments. It is interesting to find John Henry Newman (as an Anglican) saying, "Anyone who maintains that the Church is all that Christ intended her to be has the analogy of Theism full against him." (*Lectures on the Prophetical Office of the Church*, 1837, Lect. viii. p. 235.) He goes on to contend that since the Church is not now one, it is not infallible ("since the *one* has become in one sense *many*, the full prophetical idea is not now fulfilled." *Ib.* p. 239). Those who believe that even a united Church would not be infallible should be still more ready to admit that the division of Christendom into many sects, episcopal or non-episcopal, prevents any one of them claiming to be all that an ideal Church might be. The ideal Church would be, in the language of St. Augustine, a "Congregatio societasque hominum in qua fraterna charitas operetur." (*De fide et symb.* 21.)

Church, then you cannot use the Apostolical succession as an absolute criterion of the difference between a true Church and a false, or the decisions of conciliar majorities as an infallible test of divine truth, or the reception of the Holy Eucharist from a duly authorised person as an absolute test of present grace, or the sentence of a Borgia Pope or a fanatical Council as the test of a man's spiritual position in the sight of God. If this is what you want (and I do not suppose that at the present day any reflecting person does want so to apply his theory of the Church), then I admit that the doctrine of the Church's ideality is fatal to her practical value. Anyone who would take such a view would be capable no doubt of holding that an ideal is of no use because it is "only" an ideal. But, if in the moral and even in the political sphere, ideals are the "fountain light of all our day," why should it not be so in the ecclesiastical sphere also? If the individual's moral and spiritual life is made what it is by the pursuit of an ideal which can never be fully realized, why should the high and magnificent ideal which Christ's vision of His kingdom sets up before the Christian Society fail to be the very life of actual Christian communities, though no one of them at any given time and place nor all of them together can be absolutely identified with that holy city, the New Jerusalem, which the Seer of Patmos saw "coming down from God out of heaven prepared as a bride adorned for her husband?"

And now let us see how this principle—that the Church is ideal—helps us in our attitude towards the many controversies which have raged and still rage round this great question of the Church.

(1) Firstly then, there is the question of the Church's Unity. Certainly if we have any adequate conception of the Church as the organized army of God enlisted in a great crusade against the powers of evil, in the great enterprise of setting up Christ's kingdom among men, we must say that Unity belongs to the very essence of the Church — yes, outward, visible, organized Unity. That is the ideal, and an ideal which, like other ideals, we should certainly seek to make real. But when the Church is actually divided, we have no right to say that this body which has seceded from the Church is a mere Schism, while that body which has been seceded from is the true Church of Christ. Schism —schism among persons in whom there is anything left of the Christian character—is *pro tanto* injurious to the full realization of the Church idea, alike in the body that forsakes the communion of their fathers and in the body that is seceded from. Sometimes the balance of blame may be on one side, sometimes on the other, sometimes on neither, except so far as mere ignorance and error and misunderstanding are objects of blame. Schism is always an evil, but sometimes it is a duty. It is a sin only in so far as it is wilful and unnecessary. Still, however the schism originated, it is always right to make for reunion, though not for reunion at all costs. Unity is a note of the true Church, but it is not the only note. If the Church is not infallible, there may sometimes be evils worse than schism. And re-

member that just as schism is a question of degree (there may be more or less of the schismatic character about the acts of individuals or of bodies), so unity is a question of degree also. Ideal unity could certainly involve what is sometimes called corporate reunion; but, where corporate reunion is not possible except at a price too heavy to pay, then the more unity the better. Under present circumstances, while we certainly ought not to lose sight of the ideal of organized, formal, canonical unity, more unity may really be obtainable by increased intercourse, recognition, and co-operation among the formally divided fragments of Christ's Church—especially upon great moral and social questions—than by active proselytism or premature and one-sided schemes of formal amalgamation.*

(2) There is the question of the Church's office in the matter of doctrine. If we recognise the ideality of the true Church, we can attribute authority to the Church without attributing to her infallibility. The authority of the Church in the matter of doctrine means the authority of the Christian consciousness. It belongs to the mission and ideal of the Church to be the organized expression of this

* Even Newman could admit that any assembly of two or three Christians had in it something of the true Church character: "The meeting of two or three private men in Christ's name is one kind of fulfilment, and in default of higher opportunities, may be attended with a portion of divine blessing," while the highest "measures of truth," "amounting to a continual infallibility, were it ever intended, might require the presence of a superhuman charity and peace" [not merely apostolical succession, &c.], "which has never been witnessed since the disciples 'continued steadfastly in the Apostles' doctrine and fellowship,'" &c. (*l. c.* pp. 240, 241.)

consciousness: the more fully she does so, the more the Church becomes all that Christ meant His Church to be. But let us remember that, though the Spirit of God works in the Christian community, and though in due time the work of the Holy Spirit in the consciousness of the community finds expression in formal ecclesiastical changes, that work begins in the heart and intellect of individual persons. Even the Homo-ousion was the formula of a local Church before it was adopted by the Catholic Church at Nicæa, and it must have been the suggestion of an individual brain before it was received by the local Church of Palestine. And, when it was first suggested, it is likely enough that it was treated as the rash and heretical speculation of an audacious and unspiritual thinker. It is by the action of the Church, organized and formal or unorganized and informal, that the advances of Christian thought, the continual and progressive revelations which the Spirit makes to the Christian consciousness—pass from the individual soul into an abiding possession of the Christian community. The more the organized visible Church answers to her ideal, the more fully she performs this function: it is only the authority of the Church that can convert the ideas of private Theologians into the faith of a Society.

And (3) all that I have said of doctrine is equally applicable to Christian morality. We should have truer ideas of the nature of Church authority, if we thought of it more frequently in connexion with morality than in connexion with doctrine. There is, indeed, a place for authority even in the matter of doctrine. Clearly, if there were no place for authority in Christian doctrine, the great mass of non-speculative persons could not be Christians at all. There could be no such thing as Christian education, and it is clear that without Christian education Christianity could be only a phase of individual opinion: it could never be a Religion. And the same must be true of every kind of religious or of irreligious belief—even the most negative. Not to teach children that there is a God and something which we call Duty, is for all practical purposes to teach them that there is no God and no such thing as Duty. Silence is a more effective teacher of negation than denial, for denial must at least convey a knowledge of the propositions denied. Whether children believe or disbelieve, their creed will be equally, in the first instance, based upon authority. And, however high you may place the duty of subsequent enquiry and private judgment, it is obvious that the vast majority of men will alike on matters of Religion and of Morality, and even of Science or History, believe what they think is believed by the people whom they may think are likely to know. It is an exaggeration (with Mr. Balfour*) to treat all belief on authority as *wholly* non-rational. Not only may the choice of authority rest upon a rational process, but the believers may have very good reasons for the actual substance of what they believe. Only those reasons are themselves suggested by authority. It is due to the action of some form of social influence—whether it be from parent or teacher, from

* In *The Foundations of Belief.*

S

University Professor or from the diffused consensus of what the man takes to be the body of religious people or of sensible people—that the man knows of these reasons, and estimates them highly, while the reasons for any alternative belief he does not know of, or has heard mentioned in such a way that he has never fairly weighed their claims against those which came to him commended by the larger weight of authority. This is true of the beliefs of the great majority in matters of Science and Religion, but it is still more completely true of moral beliefs. If we were asked to say why the average modern Englishman condemns a host of practices in which the cultivated Greek saw no harm, and approves conduct which he would have regarded as weak, sentimental, and irrational, the answer is briefly, "Because the Christian Church—summing up in its judgments the fruits of whole centuries of moral thought and experience, and especially of the unique impetus given to moral progress by the work and teaching of Jesus the Christ—long ago bound one set of practices and loosed the other: and the Church of to-day, while in some points it has amended or supplemented the judgments of the past, still in the main, on these fundamental matters, ratifies and confirms these past judgments of the Church." That is the main reason why the average man of to-day condemns suicide, abortion, infanticide, and the like, as well as the more recently condemned practices of slavery and religious persecution; and that is why he approves on the whole in others, even when he does not practise it himself, self-denying charity towards the weak and the poor and the outcast.

No doubt it will be said that the conscience of the modern world approves or condemns these things. Quite true. It does so with greater or less vigour and independence — ranging from the merest external acquiescence to the most passionate conviction. But then this conscience of the individual is itself moulded by the society in which he lives; if his conscience is really Christian in its judgments, by the Christian society in which he has moved. In some cases his acceptance of the authoritative moral creed may be skin-deep, as appears when he takes service under a Chartered Company, and finding himself among a society of ruffians throws off the yoke of Christian civilization, and submits his private judgment to the moral code prevalent among ruffians. At other times the moral conviction is passionate and deep enough, but it is not the result of an unbiassed thinking out of the moral problems, even by a Moral Reason itself moulded by centuries of Christianity. That is a thing few of us ever attempt to do, and it is well that we do not. For the task is utterly impossible. It would be scarcely possible to discriminate fully between the part of one's ethical judgments which is due to reverence for authority, and the part which is due to the independent workings of one's own Reason; and who would trust himself to make the attempt? In speculative matters, though we all start from authority, though we never wholly escape from its influence (the influence of fashion is as plainly discernible in Philosophy as it is in the cut of a coat or the shape of a hat), yet we do partially escape from it, and it should be the effort of all good education ultimately to enable us to form our own judgments at least up to the point to which the individual's capacity and information qualify him to do so. But in moral matters, when the judgment is to such a large extent the expression of character, then the wise man will hesitate much more and much longer, before he sets up his private judgment against a consensus of good men. Of course, in pronouncing them good men he is exercising his own moral judgment. The choice of the authority, whenever it is not unconscious, is always an act of private judgment. And moral education consists very largely in emancipating the individual from the dominion of authority accepted or imposed by mere chance or external circumstance and enabling him to choose his authority on truly ethical grounds. No doubt it is the aim of all moral education to enable the man ultimately to form independent ethical judgments of his own, but that very power is acquired through a process of habituation which itself involves a continual warping and contracting of the moral judgment. We may choose our authority, as the painter chooses the school in which he studies art. It is no more possible to remain impartial in the choice between good and evil after a long course of imitation of good men and familiarity with good ideas than it is to remain impartial between beauty and ugliness after an artist's long study of great masters. And yet without that education the man would never have learned to judge at all. The original step that we took in submitting ourselves—however provisionally and with whatever reserves—to a moral master whom we took to be good, will infallibly have lessened the freedom of all future acts of choice.

In the field of morals therefore the influence of authority, and in particular of the authority of the Church, is far more directly and more demonstrably inevitable, unavoidable, and salutary than it is in the sphere of doctrine or other intellectual matters. It is no doubt desirable to cultivate the habit of forming moral judgments for ourselves and of acting upon them. But in the vast majority of cases these independent judgments will still be visibly charged —in their actual matter or content—with the influence of the society in which we have lived; and when the individual does take one of those great forward steps in which he condemns those things in which even his best contemporaries have seen no harm, or hears a new categorical imperative where they have heard it not, in that very act he is very often showing most conspicuously and most triumphantly the success of the moral education which had moulded that sensitive conscience of his. When the brave monk Telemachus leapt down into the arena and proclaimed at the cost of his life the cessation of gladiatorial combats in the now Christian Empire, that was the triumph not of an individual conscience at war with its environment, but the triumph of the collective consciousness of the Christian Church which spoke in him. Only because the best part of the Christian society had already condemned the combats, and because the very men who stoned him were secretly conscious that the thing was wrong, did that one man's act of individual loyalty to Christ and truth close that shameful chapter in the annals of humanity.

I have been trying to show how undeniable a thing has been this influence of the Christian Church in the sphere of Morals. Binding and loosing is, always has been, and always will be of the essence of the Church's work. But all the same, it is just in the case of morals that the Christian Church—interpret it how you will; any local or other section of the Church or the whole Christian Church of any one time put together—is most evidently not infallible. By attending exclusively to the formulæ used and not to the meaning which is put upon them, and by excluding from your conception of the Church the worsted minorities, it is just possible to represent the Church as infallible in the matter of doctrine. Unless we arbitrarily limit our ideas of the Church's authoritative teaching to the decisions of Councils, and thereby evacuate that idea of all present meaning, no student of ecclesiastical history can seriously contend that the Church's practical teaching on ethical questions has been always the same or always right. Put as high as you like (and I should be disposed to put very high indeed) the distinction between all Christian ethics and all ethical teaching that has been entirely uninfluenced by Christianity, yet it is surely impossible to maintain that the ideal of the "Imitatio Christi" is the same as the ideal say of that typical product of eighteenth-century Anglicanism, "The Whole Duty of Man." On particular and detailed questions of Ethics, on the host of questions connected with marriage and family relations, as to the lawfulness of War, as to the Christian's attitude to the State, to the theatre, to all manner of worldly pleasures and enjoyments, as to the right employment of property and the right treatment of the poor, as to the duty and the limits of Veracity, the attitude of the Church or of the Christian consciousness has differed frequently and widely. Now whenever authority does not amount to infallibility, it is clear that the admission of error carries with it the right of rebellion. Any theory of State authority which is now held by educated men—however high it places that authority and the duty of submission to the State—admits that that authority and that duty have limits. The very same considerations which compel submission in all ordinary cases, compel and require rebellion in the exceptional case. The higher, the more sacred the institution of the State, the more imperative the duty of obedience in ordinary cases, so much the more undeniable and the more solemn becomes the obligation of rebellion in the exceptional case. The State, like the Church, is a more or less imperfect embodiment of an Ideal. In the vast majority of cases we best show our reverence for that ideal, and help forward its realization by submission to the actual State with all its failings and shortcomings. The higher our ideal, the greater should be our reverence for the poor, halting, clumsy, corrupt, sometimes ridiculous efforts of actual communities to embody this ideal in living, concrete human organization.

But all the same this very reverence for the Ideal will now and again compel the good citizen to rebel against the actual State, when the contrast between the actual State and such an approximation of the Ideal as seems practicable under given circumstances reaches a certain intensity, though the protest may vary from passive resistance to armed rebellion.

Is it not time that we should apply a similar attitude towards the Church and the Churches? Would it not supply us with more intelligible, more natural solutions of many practical problems? We could reverence Unity, we could recognise the value of Episcopacy, without proclaiming it a duty in Spain to acquiesce in the superstitions and the falsehoods which we think it right to denounce and repudiate in England. We could recognise the Church of England as the best and most satisfactory representative for us of the true Church of Christ in this land without denying the right of the Church in Scotland to organize herself on a non-episcopal basis. We can do our utmost to promote visible Unity in England without denying that Nonconformist bodies may still be attempts—more or less successful—to realize the true Church idea, and their Ministries as more or less successful attempts to embody the true ideal of Priesthood. We can recognise the absolute necessity of a teaching Church—of Church doctrine, of formulæ or dogma—without claiming finality for any actual deliverance either of the whole Church or of any branch of it, or denying the right of the Christian consciousness, and therefore, in the first instance, of the individual to be faithful to the teaching of Science, of Criticism, of History, of enlarged and developed spiritual experience. Finally and most important of all, it would teach us to make more of the Christian Church in its relation to practical morality — to realize more alike our debt to the Church and our obligations to her—without any surrender of the right and duty of loyalty to the voice of conscience within us. There can be no progress unless human society is so organized as to mould and shape the character and conduct of individuals, so that the new moral conquests so to speak of the best men are in time registered and embodied in a social law. Equally little can there be any moral progress unless individual men will have the courage to go beyond the established conventional morality of their society in their judgments and in their conduct. Ultimately it is the moral consciousness of individuals that creates moral progress in the society.

I have left myself little time to dwell on the practical outcome of these principles in their bearing upon the conduct of the individual life: yet they have most important practical lessons. To some I know that any exaltation of authority in the sphere of practice may seem positively immoral. The doctrine of authority may of course be abused or exaggerated; it is exaggerated for instance when a writer, little enough inclined to attach importance to the judgment of the Christian Church, pronounces that to wish to be better than the world is to be already on the threshold of immorality.* It is the authority of the best men, not of the majority or of the average man, that I have tried to extol, the

* BRADLEY, *Ethical Studies*, p. 180.

authority of the best men interpreting and developing the authority which their consciences have owned in Christ. And yet after all, is not the root of the low standard of feeling and conduct on practical matters with which so many men are content, traceable precisely to this—that they trust too much to their consciences? Their religion consists, they will tell you, simply in this—in not doing what their conscience (conscience unsolicited, untrained, unenlightened) tells them to be wrong. That is what they understand by doing their duty. The duty of educating, enlightening, informing the conscience, is one which they do not recognise at all. They come up to their ideal more often perhaps than better men; it is precisely their ideal that is at fault. It never occurs to them to compare and test their ideal by higher ideals; to strive and struggle after a higher ideal; to submit themselves to all those influences by which men's ideals are elevated and their consciences made more sensitive. They do not recognise that to such a very large extent they are entrusted with the making of their own consciences; and yet they cannot make them aright without the help of higher influences outside themselves, and pre-eminently the influence of Christ and His Church. They fail to recognise that their consciences are day by day being moulded and fashioned—enlightened and quickened, or blunted and numbed—by the atmosphere which they voluntarily breathe, by the prayers that they say or leave unsaid, by the self-examination that they practise or omit, by the company they keep, by the worship and the Communions which they attend or neglect, by the books which they read, by the amusements in which they indulge, by the use which they make or neglect to make of the opportunities of their life. In a word, what they neglect is the education of Conscience; and yet it is as absurd to expect a noble life to result even from a tolerably faithful submission to the demands of an uneducated conscience as it is to suppose that we shall attain knowledge and culture by simply not wilfully setting ourselves against the claims of truth or of beauty when they happen to fall in our way, without making any effort to seek for them, and to find them.

All true education, in a sense, must be self-education; and yet it is equally true to say that all education is social. Church and State alike we ought more and more to look upon in the light of great educational institutions, in which we must seek to educate both ourselves and others,—as the two great organizations of the One Human Society whose highest end it is to realize the ideal which Christ called the Kingdom of Heaven.*

---

* It is a remarkable fact that the only instance which has reached the English press of an officer facing professional ruin and social obloquy by refusing to fight a duel was not a Protestant or secularistic champion of the rights of conscience, but a Roman Catholic, whose reverence for the Church had taught him to believe in the existence of a standard of conduct higher than the conventional practice of his class.

XVI.

PERSONALITY IN GOD AND MAN

*Myrtle Lecture in the University of Aberdeen,
February 16, 1898.*

EVERY student of ancient Philosophy is familiar with the difficulty and embarrassment manifested by the Greeks whenever they want to speak about the will. The Classical Greek writers have simply no word for expressing it, still less have they a word which will enable them to affirm or deny the existence of what the moderns call Freewill. The word αὐτεξουσία (used in this sense) is one which we owe to those strenuous assertors of freedom, the philosophically educated Greek Fathers. And a disposition to eliminate, to minimise, or to explain away this element in human nature has descended to some of the modern thinkers who owe the best that is in them to Plato and Aristotle. They attempt to analyse away the will into thought, or a combination of thought and feeling, just as their opponents, the empiricists, try to explain it away into feeling. For the purpose which I have in view it is hardly necessary to discuss the difficult psychological question whether or in what sense the will is a separate faculty, still less to enter for a single moment upon the old controversy over Freewill which is likely for an indefinite time, if not for ever, to distract and to fascinate every mind that is capable of the fierce delights of serious thinking. Those who, from the intellectualist point of view, deny that volition, or conation, is something distinct from desire taken in connection with Reason, have to admit that when we desire a thing without taking measures to obtain it, we do not desire it in the same sense in which we do when the desire leads to action. This desire that results in action is just what ordinary people call will. On the other hand, those who identify will with feeling can hardly decline, if pressed, to admit that there is an important distinction between feelings which inspire action and those which do not.

There is perhaps no direction in which some of the most recent Metaphysic shows a more decided advance than in its more definite insistence upon volition as one of the three inseparable functions of the human soul. "Whenever we are awake, we are thinking; whenever we are awake, we are willing," says Mr. Bosanquet. He naturally thought it unnecessary to add (though perhaps this undenied fact is not always remembered in some quarters) "whenever we are awake, we are feeling."* No doubt it is important to insist that these three activities imply one another, that none of them would be intelligible without the others. I will not ask whether in the lowest creatures there can be such a thing as feeling without thought; but in the adult human being, at all events, there is no such thing as feeling without

* Mr. BRADLEY's *Appearance and Reality* is still more decided on this point, however different the inferences which he draws as to the ultimate nature of reality from that which I should draw myself.

thought. We at least do not feel without knowing that we feel. Moreover, an unrelated feeling is something which we never experience. Our feelings come to us before or after other feelings, and we know that they have this relation of priority or posteriority to one another; we do not feel a pain without knowing when and where we feel it, or without being able to assign to it a more or less definite degree. Equally impossible is the attempt to get at a moment of consciousness which is pure thinking. All our thoughts are inseparably bound up with feeling, or the content of feeling. I will not dwell upon the fact (for it does not directly concern us here) that our thoughts, when they are thoughts of something actual and not of mere abstractions, are always thoughts of something which could under certain circumstances be felt, or else of something that could feel. But at least it is undeniable that the act of thinking is itself accompanied by all manner of feelings. Nobody is capable of such intellectual concentration as to be at any given moment all thought. The thinking being is always conscious of being hot or cold, conscious of a mass of feelings—of sight, of touch, and the like at every moment of his thought. Some of these feelings are so inseparable from the act of thinking that the beginner in such subjects finds it difficult to realize that the tension of the nerves, which when continued developes into a headache, is not really the thought itself and does not warrant his speaking of his mind as actually occupying a certain amount of space inside his head.

Still more vain is the attempt to isolate volition from either thought or feeling. We do not will without knowing what we will, and the imagined object which we seek to realize could not affect us unless it appealed to some kind of desire in us, and desire, though it may and must be more than feeling, is feeling. Not only have we no actual experience of either thought or feeling or volition in isolation from the other two, but none of them can be made intelligible to us apart from the other two. Each of them by itself is a mere abstraction. We have no reason to believe that a wholly thinking being, a wholly feeling, or a wholly willing being is possible. Even in the creatures below us there may, we might conjecture, be something faintly analogous to the thinking element; while the lowest appetite in the lowest sentient being seems to contain in it an element of conscious impulse which is not a mere feeling or mere thought. There may be beings above us in whom feeling and volition may be something so different from what we understand by the words, that we can only apply those terms to them as mere analogies or symbols of some higher reality, but then, if that be so with their feelings and their volitions, it must be equally so with their thoughts. To take one simple illustration of this: attention is an act of the will, and thought cannot exist without attention. Thought which went on without attention would be something very different from thought as we know it. To us thought without will is as meaningless an abstraction as the "unconscious will" of another school.

But I must check myself from straying further into these interesting problems of Psychology and Metaphysic. I hope that I have said nothing which will be unintelligible even to those (if there be such persons in an academic audience north of the Tweed) who are without an elementary knowledge or a rudimentary love for Philosophy. I want to go on to apply these truths—so simple that they are seldom explicitly denied, though they are often ignored—to certain questions of Theology and then to certain very practical questions of Religion. We have seen that it belongs to the very nature of mind to be active. In mind as we know it volition is as essential an element as thought or feeling. And if this is true of mind as we know it in man, must it not be true also of mind as we believe it to exist in God?

I must not here attempt to reproduce the arguments which lead us to think of the ultimate principle or ground or cause of all things in terms of Mind. I will only say that I believe the philosophical arguments for Theism are but a thinking out with greater thoroughness and explicitness of the reasons which actually lead the religious consciousness of the plain man up to Theism, or which satisfy his reflecting years of the truth of a creed which he has accepted on authority in childhood. When the plain man says, "The world could not have made itself: there must have been somebody to make it," he is only epitomising the Philosopher's argument that the demand of reason for a cause can only be satisfied by a rational will—that the only true cause is a final cause, and that final causes can only become efficient causes in a conscious being who unites in himself power and knowledge—in other words in a rational will. So again the plain man says there must be a God because he vaguely feels the superiority of mind to matter, and the improbability or incredibility of the production of the higher by the lower, of the development of mind in a mindless Universe. When that line of thought is worked out by a Metaphysician, it developes into the Idealist argument that matter is inconceivable, unintelligible, meaningless, apart from mind. But I must not stay to follow up these lines of thought. What I want to plead for is this—that, if you determine to interpret the Universe in terms of mind, you should do it thoroughly. Mind, as we know it, includes will and feeling as well as thought. You have no right, therefore, to think of God only as thought without thinking of Him also as feeling and as willing.

From the intellectual point of view, this Aristotelian idea of God as pure thought is based upon the apotheosis of an abstraction, and it is, I contend, a conception of God which, if thoroughly realized, would satisfy no religious or moral need of the human soul. For you must remember that this God of the Hegelians, or (I will say) of some Hegelians, is not in any sense the cause of the Universe. If that is not made quite clear by the Master, from whose voluminous writings you could no doubt quote passages which seem to afford some sanction for the idea of creation, no doubt is left about it in the writings of his disciples. Their Deity at least does not make or cause the world

T

to be what it is. He merely knows it to be what it is; he only causes the world in the sense in which you or I may be said from the Idealist point of view to "make nature"—that is to say in the sense that an object cannot exist without a subject to know it—except that he knows the whole and we know only fragmentary portions of it.

When we think of all the pain and the sorrow, the sin and the disappointment and the misery of life, perhaps we may be tempted to imagine that we are better off than such a Deity for seeing but the uttermost part of this spectacle of pain. For we can at least sympathise with the sorrow that we cannot cure, while the heartless Deity of the Hegelians can only regard it as an interesting object of intellectual contemplation. And we can do something—each of us can do something, and by union with our fellow-men we can do much—to fight against all this evil, whereas a Deity who only thinks can do nothing at all. It is true that if we knew the whole, we might be enabled to see all things working together for a final goal of good. With personal immortality that is a possible conception, but then Hegelianism rarely admits, and hardly ever insists upon, the idea of personal Immortality. And surely without Immortality for man, such a Deity, if he were capable of the sympathy and the love which Christianity has taught us to attribute to God, would (if I may say so without irreverence) spend his life in lamentation at the imperfections of the Universe to which he finds himself annexed as by some inevitable, eternal, unintelligible fate. For such a Universe might have a meaning "on the whole," but what of those whose short life ends in misery, failure, and sin? If the Hegelian Deity were capable of sympathy, surely he must sorrow with these. I have said he would spend his life: but I had forgotten that the Hegelian Deity is out of time altogether. And that reminds me that after all, in attributing to this timeless being even this one function of thought, I am attributing to him more than would be done by some of his worshippers. For, though they are clear that God is thought, they will not always allow us to say that he thinks. There have been eminent Philosophers of this School—men of whom I would speak with the profoundest respect, men to whom British Philosophy owes an incalculable debt—who certainly have believed in a God who is self-conscious; but I know also not undistinguished disciples of theirs who believe themselves to be in substantial harmony with the teaching of their Masters and who yet ridicule the idea that the Philosopher's God can have anything in common with the God of Christianity. For such men God may be thought, but he is not a thinker: he may be thought, but he comes to a consciousness of himself—he "finds himself," as the phrase is—only in the consciousness of individual mortal men. There must be something wrong surely with a Philosophy when it provides a phraseology which can be used equally and indiscriminately by those who adopt absolutely contradictory answers to the most momentous question which can possibly divide serious thinkers into opposite camps!

But I waive this question. Even when God is conceived of as a thinking Personality, how, I venture to ask, can we be the better for believing in or worshipping a will-less and unfeeling Deity? We cannot think of him as moral. Those Hegelians who do think of God as morally perfect omit to tell us what Goodness can mean in a being who does nothing, causes nothing, wills nothing; who sympathises not and loves not. Aristotle was only consistent when, with such a conception of the Deity, he ridiculed the notion that God can care whether men are good or bad, and when he urged that we become like him most when we lose ourselves in isolated, anti-social contemplation or study of nature. Even Aristotle forgot himself so far as to make pure thought capable of pleasure, and failed to observe that when he makes nature aim at the good he was bringing back that moral ideal which he had proposed to banish from his interpretation of the Universe. The word 'good' could mean nothing to us apart from the judgments of value upon which our moral activity depends. It is creditable to the heart, if not to the head, of Aristotle's Hegelian imitators that they are seldom consistent and thorough-going in the working out of their fundamental thesis, and that they will persist in bringing into some kind of ill-defined connexion with the moral life a Being to whom they theoretically refuse the essential conditions of a moral existence.

I have tried to set before you the two rival conceptions of God with which modern Philosophy is confronted, and I have tried to indicate some of the logical consequences of accepting the one which is, I fear, most in vogue among students of Philosophy at the present time—at least in the southern parts of this island. But I do not want for a moment to scare anyone away from it for fear of its practical consequences. What I do want to insist upon is the irrationality and inconsistency of first pretending to interpret the Universe in terms of mind, and then substituting for mind as we know it a one-sided abstraction of pure thought which is unlike anything that we know or have any reason to believe to be possible. The whole tendency of modern speculation confirms the natural tendency of the religious consciousness to interpret the Universe in terms of Mind. So far the Christian thinker will welcome its results; only let us have the courage to say that, if we accept so much, we will not be juggled into accepting some miserable abstraction in place of the living God by that old bugbear of philosophical polemics, the charge of anthropomorphism. Of course our God is anthropomorphic: and so must be every God whom the mind of man can really conceive. When the Hegelian speaks of God as Thought he is as anthropomorphic as we are when we insist that, if God is Mind, he must be Will and Feeling as well as Thought. Indeed, the Hegelian is more anthropomorphic than the ordinary Theologian. For the Hegelian, when he is in earnest about his Theism, always seems to assume that God's thinking is exactly the same as ours except for the fact that he comprehends all the Universe at once: whereas the Theologians have always insisted that such terms as Thought and Will and Love are always applied to God *sensu eminentiori*. We apply these terms to him because they are the highest categories that we have. We must use them or we must cease to think at all. We shall not think of God more worthily or truly by hypostatizing one side of human nature, and banishing from our conception of God all that gives his highest worth and lovableness to man. Far more philosophical is the position of the orthodox Scholasticism which declares that God is essentially a Trinity—Power, Wisdom, and Love—Father, Son, and Holy Ghost—three Persons or eternally distinguishable properties united in one indivisible Unity. Such a God too can be intelligibly conceived of as revealing himself in Man—imperfectly, progressively in the whole history of the human race, pre-eminently and supremely in Him who beheld the open vision of God as His Father and taught us by character and word and life to think of Him as being essentially Love.

This Lecture is to be devoted to some subject connected with practical Religion. So far I have been dealing with somewhat speculative matters, and yet I do not think I have been unpractical. For I do not know anything more important from the most severely practical point of view than to keep our conception of God high and pure. And therefore I do not think I have been departing from the purposes of this lecture in warning you against the imposing rhetoric in which an essentially irreligious and unchristian conception of God is sometimes so skilfully disguised as to deceive the very elect. But I go on to the more directly practical application of my subject. In Religion as in Theology—on the subjective side as on the objective—there is a danger in a one-sided insistence on any of these three aspects of spiritual being, knowledge or feeling or will.

We know the danger of substituting intellectual speculation or the mere acceptance of an intellectual Creed for practical Religion. It was exhibited by the early Gnostic heresies which hovered between an unsocial asceticism and a sensual antinomianism. It has been exhibited all through the Church's history by that paralysis of spiritual life which ensues when the acceptance of dogma is taken to be an end in itself instead of simply a means to a holy life. It is exhibited in its way by the modern mode of thought to which I have already alluded, which, in spite of the high spiritual aims of many of its representatives, does tend towards substituting an attitude of self-satisfied contemplation of things in general for the attitude of antagonism towards moral evil. Man is apt to become like the God whom he worships. Thinking of God as a mere contemplator of all time and all existence must tend to substitute in ourselves an attitude of interested and amused contemplation of evil for the attitude of strenuous resistance to it. There is a danger lest we should end, like such men as Renan, in regarding human sin and human misery as simply adding something to the piquancy of the cultivated man's self-centred survey of an eminently curious Universe.

And so with the one-sided effort to make the religious life centre or terminate in feeling. When it is supposed that salvation consists essentially in a certain state of emotion, in comfortable experiences, in inward peace or the like and not in a certain state of will, we are already on the high road to moral and social apathy. No doubt it is in religious and social emotion that we must seek for the springs of religious and social life. True faith, as the sober teachers of justification by faith have always taught, is the faith that works by love. The conversion of the heart means conversion of the will. Nor can there be a real love of God whom we have not seen without a love of the brethren whom we have seen. But, when all the stress of religious teaching is laid upon the emotional state and the reference of this state to the will is forgotten, the feeling that is cultivated by such teaching is apt itself to degenerate into a kind of feeling which is by no means always fruitful in good works. Some of us have been reminded of the possibility of such degradation of true religious emotion by the picture drawn in the life of Tennyson of the old aunt whose eyes streamed with tears as she spoke of the goodness of God who had eternally damned all those nearest and dearest to her and predestined her, no better than the rest, to everlasting salvation. It is very likely that this particular old lady was a kindly old woman enough, who did not in the least realize the awful meaning of the conventional language she was using. But the history of Religion is full of indications of the natural tendency of such wholly individualistic religious ideals to realize themselves in the lives of those by whom they are absorbed. In recent times we may perhaps find a more formidable danger in the tendency of mere æstheticism to clothe itself in the language of spiritual edification. The school in question is right when it teaches that the enjoyment of beautiful things is an element of the ideal life. But when we find a recent thinker suggesting that the listening to instrumental music is becoming the only rational form of worship, we cannot but suspect a tendency to degrade moral goodness—the right direction of the will—from the supreme place which it ought to occupy in the scale of spiritual values in favour of mere emotional exaltation. At all events, in more vulgar minds there is a tendency beneath the specious names of self-realization or culture to cast a halo of spiritual blessedness over what is simply a refined way of amusing ourselves. Amusement has its due place in life, the noblest kinds of amusement have a very high place indeed; but we shall give it more than its right place if we suppose that we can sanctify an existence divided between continental lounging and questionable French novels by calling it devotion to the sacred study of Art.

Lastly, there may be such a thing as a one-sided insistence upon the importance of the will in the religious life. Of all the three exaggerations, this is to my mind the least dangerous. For essentially we are in the right when we say that Religion consists in a certain state of the will. We can only exaggerate this doctrine when we forget the essential connexion of the state of our wills with the ideas or ideals that dominate our thoughts and the emotional states which determine the character of our desires. "The stern daughter of the voice of God," writes Lord Tennyson, "unclothed with the warmth of the feelings, is as impotent to convert as the old Stoicism."

There is no shallower idea, again, than to suppose that what we believe has no effect on what we will, or that the state of our wills has no effect on what we believe. Our moral ideal itself is a kind of belief—the most important of all beliefs; and yet who will say that the ideal does not reveal the character—the habitual direction or bent of the man's will? Our moral ideal is the belief which is most closely connected with the will: this is the belief which most of all it rests with our wills to hold fast or to let go. But there are many other beliefs which have a powerful influence upon conduct, and which in greater or less degree are connected with the state of our wills. Creed and character act and react upon one another.

What then, you may ask, is the practical outcome of these facts? I do not mean for one moment to urge anyone to stifle intellectual doubt for fear of its practical consequences; nor do I mean to suggest that a man is necessarily a bad man because he is for a time or even permanently unable to accept the Christian or the Theistic view of the Universe. It would indeed be immoral to try to believe things which seem to us contrary to reason or unsupported by evidence, if only we give a sufficiently wide extension to our idea of "evidence." But a very little study of the evidence for Theism will assure you that in the ordinary sense of the word there can hardly be said to be "evidence" either for or against Theism. The most that can be shown is that Theism is the hypothesis about the ultimate nature of things which fits and explains the facts better than any other. Now if we were dealing with purely speculative or scientific matters, we should of course accord to our hypothesis only just the amount of weight which was warranted by its probability. This attitude of suspended judgment becomes impossible when belief calls for action. And even in purely scientific matters it is just in proportion as we find any hypothesis to give us the power of prevision or any other kind of power over nature, just when we find that a hypothesis will *work*, that we may most truly be said to believe it. Practical acceptance of a belief is no doubt consistent with speculative doubt, but even in the scientific sphere it may be said that our willingness to act upon an hypothesis is the measure of our belief in its truth.

Now for certain purposes I think we ought to treat belief in God as a working hypothesis. I do not wish to attenuate the degree of speculative certainty with which the existence of God is capable of being established. To some of us there may be no speculative doubt about it except what is implied by the necessity of admitting that it involves difficulties which we cannot altogether explain. But then there are probably minds, especially among the unmetaphysical, to which it will present itself rather as a highly probable hypothesis, and what I want to urge is, that if there seems to you a probability in its favour, and if you find it to be the belief that will serve as a guide to the noblest kind of life, the belief that inspires action best, that keeps alive most fully the sense of moral responsibility, that gives you the highest view of the possibilities of the world in which you are called upon to work—then you are absolutely entitled to believe it. Do not be afraid or ashamed of admitting that you believe because you choose to believe, because you find it an hypothesis which spiritually works.

So far you will be only doing what the man of Science does when he adopts as a working hypothesis the theory which has given him, as far as his present experience goes, the greatest command over nature for the purposes both of further knowledge and of further command over nature. But here comes a difference. The practical acceptance of a scientific belief for scientific purposes can hardly be said to involve the direction of feeling and emotion into one groove. You can use your hypothesis even at the moment when you are most inclined to doubt its finality, though I suspect that in practice it is the enthusiast for the new theory rather than the sceptic who will do most for that further investigation which will either confirm or displace it. But this is not so with our practical acceptance of the religious hypothesis. Religious feeling does not, indeed, demand the extinction of speculative open-mindedness; but it does demand the habitual dwelling upon the truth which it accepts, the habitual exclusion of the contrary hypothesis from our practical working life. For the working creed to have its practical effect upon the mind, it must dominate not merely the outward action but the habitual tone of thought, the emotions, the affections, the desires. It is precisely by exciting and maintaining these emotions that religious belief affects conduct.

Let me illustrate what I mean by two examples.

You are trying to climb a difficult mountain. You do not know which is the best way to the top. You will certainly never get there if you wait till it is proved which way will lead there. You must take what seems to you the more probable course and keep on persistently. You would fail if you refused to start till the evidence for your hypothesis was complete: you would fail still more certainly and disastrously if you kept wandering about from one path to another or attempting to strike some mean course between them. You must act as if you knew that the way you are going on was right until you see a definite reason for retracing your steps. That is what Bishop Butler meant by his doctrine that probability is the guide of life;* and your chances of success will be all the greater in proportion to the emotional confidence with which you dismiss from your minds the possibility of your being wrong. Or if the kind of emotional confidence which in such a case you place in the truth of your hypothesis seems to you a poor and inadequate parallel to the confidence which Christianity invites you to repose in Christ and the God whom He reveals, I will suggest an analogy which may be thought more adequate—the trust that we place in persons. To the metaphysical thinker the very existence of another human being besides himself is but an hypothesis — an enormously probable hypothesis because it so completely explains the facts. But there are other hypotheses which will do that;

* There is a new and a very striking restatement of this doctrine in Professor JAMES' admirable work, *The Will to Believe.*

Solipsism is an hypothesis which can never be positively disproved. And yet surely no friendship was ever dulled or dimmed by the thought that the very existence of your friend was only an hypothesis. And when you go on to examine the logical basis of your belief in your friend's character, still more evident is it that your estimate of him is after all only an hypothesis for which there is a greater or less probability. In the beginning of your friendship you acted on a belief in his goodness, or whatever the qualities were that attracted you to him, which went considerably in advance of the evidence. Even in the most reserved dealings with strangers we have to make a certain venture of faith. The most ordinary social intercourse would be frozen at its very source if we did not assume something more than was proved about the people we meet. And when we attempt to exercise spiritual influence on others, does not success very largely depend upon a willingness to believe the best of people, which not merely runs ahead of positive knowledge but implies a voluntary putting aside of much to which experience might seem to point?

Of course this provisional acceptance of an hypothesis about others falls very far short of what I mean to suggest as a parallel to our trust in God. And yet when our reasons for believing in a person's good qualities reach a certain point—a point falling very far short of scientific demonstration (for history tells us that men are often less good and friends less faithful than they seem), our confidence in them and our love of them does reach an intensity to which the most complete mathematical demonstration or the most overwhelming accumulation of experiential evidence would be capable of adding nothing. There is therefore nothing cold-hearted or cold-blooded in the admission that our belief in God can only rest speculatively upon a certain degree of probability. There is nothing in it which is in the least calculated to cloud the most ardent faith or to cool the warmest love. It was not a cynic or a sceptic who defined faith as a voluntary certainty concerning things absent.

Before I conclude, I should like to elicit from these brief reflections on the place of the will in our religious life a few definite practical counsels. I would say, then—

(1) If you determine to accept the spiritual interpretation of the world, be thorough with it. Think of God as willing and feeling, as Power and Love, and not as Thought only. Think of Him and treat Him as a Person to whom you can pray.

(2) Regard the state of the will as the most important thing in your religious life. To aim at the highest that you know, that is the most important element in Religion. *That* you may always secure, whatever turn your speculative ideas may take. But do not forget that some views as to the ultimate nature of things supply a better support and basis for this moral effort than others, and do not be afraid to adopt the Creed which seems to you to supply the most rational basis for the highest and most sustained moral effort, because you admit that the speculative reasons in its favour only amount to a greater or less degree of probability.

And (3) remember that belief can only influence conduct when it dominates the emotions: and remember further that emotion can be cultivated. Friendships die and wither (at least in their earlier stages) unless they are sustained by personal intercourse. No enthusiasm of humanity could remain undimmed by the life of an anchorite. And so if we want to make the sense of God's presence a living reality to us, if we want to make our belief in His goodness the inspiration of our lives, if we want to make the belief in Immortality a source of hopefulness and strength, then we must think on these things. We must cultivate the sense of these things by prayer and by worship, by the study of the best thoughts of the best men, whether in the Bible or out of the Bible, by frequenting (if I may so say) the society of those among the living and the departed, in whom we see most fully realized the ideal relation of God to Man, and especially by constantly keeping before our mental gaze the image of that consciousness in which we believe the ideal of Sonship to have been realized in an altogether unique and pre-eminent way. Frequent, deliberate communion with God as He has been revealed in Christ is the road to the knowledge and the love which inspire a Christian will.

www.ingramcontent.com/pod-product-compliance
Lightning Source LLC
Chambersburg PA
CBHW031247250426
43672CB00029BA/1374